Educating Ethical Leaders
for the Twenty-First Century

Educating Ethical Leaders
for the Twenty-First Century

EDITED BY
Walter Earl Fluker

CASCADE *Books* • Eugene, Oregon

EDUCATING ETHICAL LEADERS FOR THE TWENTY-FIRST CENTURY

Copyright © 2013 Wipf and Stock Publishers. All rights reserved. Except for brief quotations in critical publications or reviews, no part of this book may be reproduced in any manner without prior written permission from the publisher. Write: Permissions, Wipf and Stock Publishers, 199 W. 8th Ave., Suite 3, Eugene, OR 97401.

Cascade Books
An Imprint of Wipf and Stock Publishers
199 W. 8th Ave., Suite 3
Eugene, OR 97401

www.wipfandstock.com

ISBN 13: 978-1-62032-262-8

Cataloging-in-Publication data:

    Educating ethical leaders for the twenty-first century / edited by Walter Earl Fluker ; Foreword by Walter E. Massey.

    xvi + 116 p. ; 23 cm. Includes Bibliographical references.

    ISBN 13: 978-1-62032-262-8

    1. Leadership. 2. African American leadership. 3. Ethics. 4. Leadership—Religious aspects—Christianity. 5. Morehouse College (Atlanta, Ga.). I. Walter E. Fluker (1951–). II. Massey, Walter E. III. Title.

BV4597.53 L43 E40 2013

Manufactured in the USA

To Ingrid Saunders Jones,

Senior Vice President of Global Community Connections,

the Coca-Cola Company,

and Chairperson of the Coca-Cola Foundation,

whose visionary leadership and unwavering support made this

project possible

One of the great liabilities of history is that all too many people fail to remain awake through great periods of social change.

—Martin Luther King Jr., *Where Do We Go From Here? Chaos or Community*

Contents

Foreword by Walter E. Massey / ix
Preface / xi
List of Contributors / xiv

1 Strategies and Resources for Ethical Leadership Education in the Twenty-First Century / 1
   WALTER EARL FLUKER

2 The Ethical Dilemma in Affirmative Action Status / 38
   DERRICK BELL

3 Ethical Leadership for the Twenty-First Century: Science, Technology, and Public Policy / 51
   SHIRLEY ANN JACKSON

4 Ethics and Leadership: The Challenge of Globalization / 62
   JAMES A. JOSEPH

5 Challenging the Status Quo for Ethical Leadership / 77
   MELVINIA KING and BRYANT MARKS

6 The Role of Ethical Behavior in the Elimination of Disparities in Health / 91
   DAVID SATCHER

Contents

    7 Some Thoughts on Black Leadership / 99
        TAVIS SMILEY

    8 The Decline of Friendship in Modernity: Issues and Challenges for Ethical Leadership / 104
        PRESTON KING

Foreword

FROM ITS FOUNDING IN 1867 as an institution for the education of newly freed slaves for leadership roles in the United States following emancipation, Morehouse College has always taken the education of leaders seriously. With a history that includes the graduation of such transformational leaders as Maynard Jackson and Martin Luther King Jr., as well as countless other men who, while not as well known, have contributed so much to the betterment of society, the college has earned a reputation for being a place where leadership begins.

My first encounter with this tradition was as a student in the 1950s when Benjamin Mays was president. Although we were still in the depths of the period of rigid racial segregation, the message we heard as students every week in class assembly was that we could achieve any position in society if we dedicated ourselves to the task. Moreover, as beneficiaries of a Morehouse education, we had an obligation to aim for the highest level of success; our success being measured by what we contributed to society, not what we gained. This message was not limited to the assembly or "chapel" as it was known but was reinforced in the classroom, the dormitories, and elsewhere. We were expected to be leaders in whatever field and endeavor we pursued.

When I returned to Morehouse as president in 1995, I was very pleased—but not surprised—that this ethos still infused the campus. However, the institution was now much larger and in many ways more complex, and was committed to educating students for a much different, and in many respects more challenging, society than it was back in the 1950s. It was no longer feasible for one individual, such as Benjamin Mays, to infuse the institution with the concepts of leadership that were needed for a rapidly changing, much more global environment. Fortunately, a few thoughtful and insightful faculty members, led by Professor Willis "Butch" Sheftall, saw that the college needed a new institutionalized broad-based approach

Foreword

for engaging in discussions and developing approaches to leadership education. Thus was borne the idea for the Leadership Center at Morehouse College. The center was envisaged as a place dedicated to intellectual discourse among faculty members and students from all disciplines, as well as a place where visitors from outside Morehouse could grapple with notions of leadership in their areas of study and expertise.

The seminal step towards realizing this vision was the recruitment by Provost John Hopps of Walter Earl Fluker to be the first director of the Leadership Center in 1998. Under Professor Fluker's leadership, the center has stimulated enhanced conversations about leadership from numerous perspectives and for different audiences, from pre-college students in summer programs, to the general public through the Coca-Cola Lecture Series presented in this volume.

This volume of essays is a reflection of the multidisciplinary approach to leadership development that the center has embraced. These lectures, by leaders from fields ranging from science to law, capture the challenges leaders face, and identify the skills, attributes, and qualities that are needed to surmount these challenges. I am certain that this volume will be a valuable resource to teachers and students, and to anyone interested in understanding what it takes to be a leader in the twenty-first century.

As Walter Earl Fluker notes in his preface, the center would not have been possible without the support of many generous and supportive organizations and individuals. However, a special thanks is due to Ingrid Saunders Jones, whose support from the beginning of this effort was so important and meaningful.

WALTER E. MASSEY
President, School of the Art Institute of Chicago
President Emeritus of Morehouse College (1995–2007)

Preface

DURING MY TENURE AS Executive Director of the Leadership Center and Coca-Cola Professor of Leadership Studies at Morehouse College, I was privileged to host the Annual Coca-Cola Leadership Lecture Series. The selected lectures in this volume are part of that series, with the exceptions of the essay by Melvinia King and Bryant Marks, and my opening essay. For making the series possible I am enormously grateful to the Coca-Cola Foundation, Ms. Ingrid Saunders Jones, and Ms. Helen Smith-Price. Ms. Jones, to whom this volume is dedicated, was resolute in support of this project and indispensable to its success. In addition to serving as Senior Vice President of Global Community Connections for the Coca-Cola Company and Chair of the Coca-Cola Foundation, Ms. Jones leads the Coca-Cola Company's philanthropy efforts. Under her leadership, the company has contributed more than $466 million to support sustainable community initiatives, including the United Negro College Fund, Hispanic Scholarship Fund, Catalyst, the Critical Difference for Women program at Ohio State University, Boys and Girls Clubs of America, and the World Wildlife Fund, to name just a few. The foundation also funds The Coca-Cola First Generation Scholarship Program for first-generation college students.

A very special thanks is also extended to Dr. Walter E. Massey, former president of Morehouse College, and to the indefatigable staff of the Leadership Center. I would also like to express my thanks to Dr. Patricia Mitchell, Scholar-in-Residence at Morehouse College; Ms. Alexis Felder, Research Assistant at Boston University; and Ms. Silvia Glick, who was responsible for the final editing of the manuscript.

The contributors to this book come from a wide range of fields, including academia, law, and medicine. However, they all share the belief that ethical leadership education is necessary in order to provide the next

Preface

generation of leaders with the tools that they will need to successfully navigate the challenges of today and of the coming decades.

The book comprises eight essays. In the first, I introduce the topic of ethical leadership education and address specific strategies and resources for its implementation. Seven essays follow my piece, each addressing the topic of ethical leadership education from the unique point of view of each contributor.

Following the introductory essay, the late Derrick Bell, the first black tenured professor at Harvard Law School, discusses affirmative action and the myths surrounding it. He argues that racism is at the center of our society, notwithstanding the progress that has been made since *Brown v. Board of Education*. Using the technique of parable, he illustrates how the intransigence of structural injustice disallows true equality in universities, corporations, and other institutions.

Physicist, educator, and presidential advisor Shirley Ann Jackson discusses leadership skills from a scientist's perspective. A former chairman of the Nuclear Regulatory Commission, Dr. Jackson made decisions that impacted the health and well-being of many. Dr. Jackson describes the six principles that she considers when faced with a leadership issue. These principles involve integrity, vision, courage, action, language choice, and engaging others in decision making.

Ambassador James Joseph urges us to stop fearing globalization, and to understand that globalization is the way of the future. In the language of Joseph Nye, former dean of the Kennedy School at Harvard University, he asserts that nations and their leaders should exercise soft power rather than hard power. Hard power involves force and violence and is not a viable solution to the world's challenges. While national self-interest is the legitimate prerogative of any nation, leaders run the risk of forfeiting that right through aggression and dominance by military and economic cooptation. Joseph counsels that ethical leaders learn the art of soft power, which operates through attraction, influence, and negotiation that appeal to the highest in others' cultures and political values; and develop foreign policies that are legitimate and have moral authority. Soft power is a more reasonable and potentially productive course of action because it requires that leaders learn to listen deeply to the unpopular voices in our society that seek diverse ways of understanding. Finally, soft power allows us to connect with others in places of strategic interest.

Professors Melvinia King and Bryant Marks describe the Coca-Cola Pre-College Leadership Program at Morehouse College, which is designed to introduce high school students to the traits, skills, and behaviors necessary for ethical leadership in the twenty-first century. The program has demonstrated effectiveness in strengthening the skills that these young people will need on their road to becoming ethical leaders. These skills include the virtues, values, and virtuosities (excellences) in the Ethical Leadership Model® outlined in the introductory essay, "Educating Leaders for the Twenty-First Century: Strategies and Resources for Ethical Leadership Education."

Moving to the world of healthcare, we have an essay by former Surgeon General David Satcher, who directs the Satcher Health Leadership Institute at Morehouse School of Medicine. Dr. Satcher considers the qualities that are needed by leaders in the healthcare sector. He concludes that society needs ethical leaders who will work to change the social determinants of health—the conditions in which people are born, learn, grow, work, and age. We need ethical leaders, Satcher contends, who will take on the problems of poverty, racism, and lack of access to healthcare.

Bestselling author and talk-show host Tavis Smiley sums up the attributes that are needed by Black leaders in three words: courage, conviction, and commitment. However, while recognizing that "Black leadership" has a unique style stemming from a history of struggle, he contends that "Black leadership" is essentially no different than "leadership." He asserts that whether or not one is a leader is not dependent on race, gender, or age.

The last of the contributions is by Preston King, a professor of political philosophy and scholar-in-residence at the Leadership Center at Morehouse College, who approaches the question of leadership by an unlikely path. Professor King is concerned about the consequences of the virtual disappearance of friendship in the public realm. He believes that the absence of the ideal of friendship from public discourse negatively affects the quality of leadership.

Together, these essays advance our understanding of the challenge and promise of ethical leadership education, as we continue with the important work ahead.

Contributors

Derrick Bell (1930–2011) was the first black tenured professor at Harvard Law School and a pioneer of critical race theory, which explores the ways that racism is embedded in laws and legal institutions. His 1973 book, *Race, Racism and American Law*, is a staple in law schools throughout the United States.

Walter Earl Fluker is the Martin Luther King, Jr. Professor of Ethical Leadership and the editor of The Howard Thurman Papers Project at Boston University School of Theology. He is author of *Ethical Leadership: The Quest for Character, Civility, and Community*, and editor of *The Papers of Howard Washington Thurman*, Volume 1: *My People Need Me*, and Volume 2, *"Christian, Who Calls Me Christian?"*

Shirley Ann Jackson has been President of Rennselaer Polytechnic Institute since 1999, and was Chairman of the US Nuclear Regulatory Commission from 1995 to 1999. She serves on the President's Council of Advisers on Science and Technology and on the International Security Advisory Board, which advises the US Department of State on issues such as arms control, disarmament, and international security.

James A. Joseph is Professor of the Practice of Public Policy at Duke University and Executive Director of the United States–Southern Africa Center for Leadership and Public Values, which is based in Durham, North Carolina, and in Cape Town. He has served four US presidents, and was the first and only US ambassador to present his credentials to President Nelson Mandela.

Melvinia King is Assistant Professor of Leadership Studies and Director of the Leadership Studies Program at Morehouse College, and a member of the Policy Working Group of the African Presidential Archives and

Contributors

Research Center at Boston University. She is the author of *The African American Moral Tradition as a Resource for Leadership Education: Developing Ethical Leaders for America*.

Preston King is Visiting Professor of Political Philosophy in the Department of Political Science at Morehouse College and at the Leadership Center at Morehouse. He coedited, with Walter Earl Fluker, *Black Leaders and Ideologies in the South: Resistance and Non-Violence*, and is currently working on a sustained philosophical analysis of the locus and role of friendship in postmodern society and polity.

Bryant Marks is Assistant Professor of Psychology at Morehouse College and head of the Morehouse Male Initiative, which is a college-level effort to measure the impact of the Morehouse experience on the college's students. His research interests include the psychological impact of the Black College experience, the impact of activated stereotypes on performance and behavior, gender stereotypes among African Americans, and racial identity as a predictor of academic achievement and self-esteem.

Walter E. Massey has been President of the School of the Art Institute of Chicago since 2010 and was President of Morehouse College from 1995 to 2007. He has served as Provost and Senior Vice President for Academic Affairs of the University of California system, Professor of Physics and Dean of the College at Brown University, Professor of Physics and Vice President of Research at the University of Chicago, Director of the Argonne National Laboratory, and Director of the National Science Foundation under President George H. W. Bush. He is currently a trustee of the Andrew W. Mellon Foundation, Chairman of the Board of the Salzburg Global Seminar, and member of the board of McDonald's.

David Satcher, MD, is Director of the Satcher Health Leadership Institute at Morehouse School of Medicine. He was Surgeon General of the United States from February 1998 to August 2002; and from February 1998 until January 2001, he served concurrently as Assistant Secretary for Health at the US Department of Health and Human Services.

Tavis Smiley is host of the late-night television talk show *Tavis Smiley* on PBS and *The Tavis Smiley Show*, a one-hour weekly radio show distributed by Public Radio International. Smiley is a *New York Times* bestselling author, and his most recent book (coauthored with Cornel West) is *The Rich and the Rest of Us: A Poverty Manifesto*.

– 1 –

Strategies and Resources for Ethical Leadership Education in the Twenty-First Century

WALTER EARL FLUKER

Introduction

THE PURPOSE OF THIS introductory essay is to address the theme, "Strategies and Resources for Ethical Leadership Education."[1] The contributors to this book all address an aspect of this theme from their own area of expertise. The problem involves: (1) significant issues and challenges confronting leaders, students, and educators from many different backgrounds, cultures, and communities at the intersection of *lifeworlds* and *systems*[2] who must negotiate the difficult matters of empathy, respect, and appreciation of difference; and (2) the development of ethical student leaders and educators within specific environments who will promote habits and practices that create communities of discourse and practice that

---

1. Throughout this essay, I borrow heavily from my own work: Fluker, *Ethical Leadership*; and Fluker, "At the Intersection Where Worlds Collide."

2. Habermas, *Theory of Communicative Action*.

address the challenges of diversity and culture. A methodological approach for the infusion of culture and diversity in ethical leadership education will be proposed that utilizes three interrelated concepts and practices of *character*, *civility*, and *community* in the development of ethical student leaders.

The Problem of Diversity and Culture in Ethical Leadership Education

The basic argument of the proposed infusion strategy is that human development requires a moral anchor, a psychosocial structure in which students themselves must be central participants. The almost absolute focus on self (distinguished from a healthy sense of self, which I discuss later on) and the adoption of destructive behaviors; poor decision making and life skills; arrested development in emotional intelligence and communication skills; severe limitations in conduct; and the absence of trust, duty, and responsibility to others are all signs of an *unanchored* ethical center. In respect to diversity and culture, I argue that the ethical center both forms and informs the student's sense of self in relation to others and to his or her larger universe of discourse. Any leadership education program that seeks to spark a transformation of consciousness regarding the problem of difference must first help students engage and repair their ethical centers. In "Challenging the Status Quo for Ethical Leadership," Melvinia King and Bryant Marks give us a concrete example of the applied strategy of ethical leadership training with a racially nondiverse cohort of precollege students at Morehouse College. They describe a training program that was designed to introduce the participants to the traits, skills, and behaviors necessary for ethical leadership. A comparison of evaluations administered to the participants before and after the program, which was based on my Ethical Leadership Model®, showed that the training strengthened the skills that individuals need to be ethical leaders. The challenge going forward will be to conduct similar programs with diverse populations of students and educators, and to assess the effectiveness of such programs for measuring empathy, respect, and a sense of justice.

Diversity is not the simple amalgamation of multiculturalism and of differences in language, beliefs, disability, race, gender, class, religion, age, and medical condition; diversity covers a broad and complex spectrum of difference borne of cultural origins, ways of learning, sexual orientation, and most important for our purposes, ways of "facing the other."[3] Emphasis in the proposed strategy is placed on the concept of *difference* as a way of identifying what is at stake in developing *morally anchored character*,[4] *transformative acts of civility*,[5] and *a sense of community*[6] that seeks just relations and openness to "the other."

Issues and Challenges That Impact Diversity and Culture in Leadership Education

Fundamental to our approach is the need to address the issues and challenges that impact diversity and culture within a clearly articulated conceptual framework that can be utilized to strengthen and transform leadership education. Such an approach must support the infusion of diversity and cultural learning into leadership education.

A number of historical and contemporary issues impact this topic area. One of our contributors directs our attention to the questions that arise from the debate on the merits of affirmative action. The late Derrick Bell, in "The Ethical Dilemma in Affirmative Action Status," points out that the purpose and meaning of affirmative action are often misunderstood. In Bell's essay on institutional racism, affirmative action, and the continuing struggle for racial justice, he notes that when liberals proclaim that affirmative action is necessary to promote diversity, this allows them to avoid an examination of past and present racism. But affirmative action is not about achieving diversity or multiculturalism per se; rather, it is necessary to remedy the effects of racism—the racism inextricably bound up with the history of powerful institutions in this country. Thus, affirmative action is compensation for a wrong. For Bell, it is important, therefore, that leadership education acknowledges the many facets of affirmative action: the myths and the misconceptions surrounding it, the justifications for it, and the consequences for those who are perceived as benefitting from it.

---

3. Levinas, *Difficult Freedom*.

4. Thomas, *Living Morally*.

5. Carter, *Civility*; Etzioni, *The New Golden Rule*; Fluker, *Stones*; Goldfarb, *Civility and Subversion*; King and Devere, *The Challenge to Friendship*; Putnam, *Bowling Alone*.

6. Capra, *The Web of Life*; Devall and Sessions, *Deep Ecology*; Nhat Hanh, *Living Buddha*; Dalai Lama XIV, *Ethics*; King, *Where Do We Go From Here*; Lerner, *Politics of Meaning*; Shields and Bredemeier, *Can Sports Build Character?*; Thurman, *Search for Common Ground*.

Other issues include social-historical contexts; for example, the changing landscape of the United States in respect to the particular issues of immigration, language, religion, culture, race, poverty, class, and aesthetic ideals disseminated through communications media and educational practice. "The census calculates that by 2042, Americans who identify themselves as Hispanic, black, Asian, American Indian, Native Hawaiian and Pacific Islander will together outnumber non-Hispanic whites. Four years ago, officials had projected the shift would come in 2050."[7] Global change[8] is another major issue affecting the way that culture and diversity are incorporated into leadership education. In "Ethics and Leadership: The Challenge of Globalization," Ambassador James Joseph argues that it is increasingly important that leaders understand how to face the challenges posed by the diversity of other nations, as globalization takes on greater importance in the coming decades. Also, American leaders must consider the lessons to be learned from understanding how other societies have managed the challenges of multiculturalism. For example, South Africa has much to teach us about reconciliation, and how the value of reconciliation has been "infused into the political culture of those who govern, the theology of those who claim a new moral authority, and the ancestral tradition of those who now have the lead in building a new society."

Most models of character education, for instance, begin with traditional (virtue-based), developmental (cognitive approaches emphasizing reason and judgment), and emotional intelligence strategies (ethics of care or compassion, attachment, and spirituality) for assessment and evaluation of the self as the primary locus for impact and transformation of behavior. While nearly all models acknowledge the interaction of self in the context of social interaction with others, most, including the work of Lawrence Kohlberg and "just community" strategies, virtue ethics, and noncognitivist approaches, continue to wrestle with analytic presuppositions and protocol that borrow from the notion of an individuated self that seeks understanding and motivational resources for moral judgment and behavior in variable situations.[9] While these approaches have proven helpful in the complex and developing literature of character education, the focus on the individual actually colludes against the goal of cultural enrichment and

---

7. Roberts, "In a Generation."

8. Appiah, *Cosmopolitanism*; Friedman, *The World is Flat*; Zakaria, *Post-American World*.

9. Wren, "Philosophical Moorings."

diversity.[10] Human beings, especially our students and emerging leaders, are not discrete individuals without connection to larger social-historical narratives and traditions that define character in the context of particular communities of discourse and practice. Our approach takes its cue from all three prevalent theoretical models (cognitivist, virtue, and emotional) with emphasis on communities of discourse and practice that collide at the intersections of classrooms and public environments and emphasizes the role of spirituality and cultural imagination (the many cultural narratives, myths, rituals, and aesthetic triggers) that inform experiential and reflective learning, critical thinking, and moral judgment.[11]

I wish to be clear that our emphasis on spiritual and cultural imagination in leadership education is not necessarily an issue of religion. It is essentially an issue of attending to the human spirit, with emphasis on what it means to be human. Discussions of spirituality cover a broad and increasingly complex spectrum of beliefs, practices, and approaches within and beyond traditional religious circles. For our purposes, *spirituality* refers to a way or ways of seeking or being in relationship with the other who is believed to be worthy of reverence and highest devotion. In this definition, I am concerned with the *other* as inclusive of both individuality and community. The other is not impersonal but intimately related to who I am and who I become. According to Emmanuel Levinas,[12] the other has a *face*—and the face of the other is the foundation of ethics and the origin of civil society. Beyond our private quests for meaning and authenticity, we are connected to others. Indeed, in order to be fully human and ethical, we must "face the other." The face of the other is encountered in everyday life, but also in its strangeness and difference, in its force of obligation and interdependence. "The face of man is the medium through which the invisible in him becomes visible and enters into commerce with us."[13] In her essay, "Ethical Leadership for the Twenty-First Century: Science, Technology, and Public Development," Dr. Shirley Jackson asks us to consider ethical decision making around drug development and the regulation of nuclear power. Leaders must make decisions concerning those who may be consid-

---

10. Gallien and Jackson, "Character Development"; Lehr, et al., "Character Education"; Smagorinsky and Taxel, *The Discourse of Character Education*; Wren and Mendoza, "Cultural Identity."

11. Tisdell, "New Millenium"; Welch, *Sweet Dreams*.

12. Levinas, *Difficult Freedom*.

13. Ibid.

ered "invisible," but who in fact are real human beings, with faces that we must see in order that they be made real.

Methodological Considerations

Critical to the proposed infusion strategy of diversity and culture is the solicitation and utilization of stories in nurturing the human spirit. Stories provide the vehicles through which students come to appreciate and empathize with others. Remembering, retelling, and reliving of stories encourage the cultivation of listening or what scholars such as Stephen Carter have called *civil listening*.[14] The imagination is engaged in story discourse at two levels. One is the narrative level where the hearer is engaged in second-order discourse that is primarily descriptive and easily accessible. At a deeper level, however, there is a dimension of story that scholars have called *first order language*, which is primal and primordial; and invites the listener into a sphere of possibility that has significant implications for the student's ability to envision a future of diversity accentuating respect, tolerance, and appreciation of difference.[15]

Storytelling in the proposed model is the prime vehicle for transmission of the wisdom, habits, and practices that shape the moral character (character), transformative civil discourse (civility), and reconciling acts of community (community) of ethical student leaders. The triadic interplay of character, civility, and community will receive more attention, but it is important to point out here that the Ethical Leadership Model® discussed below takes into account that a sense of justice is paramount for leadership education and training and that even justice must find its ultimate fulfillment in compassion that is demonstrated through reconciling acts of community, which takes more than blind obedience to rules and traditions. When revitalized with imagination, tradition becomes a discourse (oral, written, or expressed through ritual) that is able to bring disclosure of personal and collective meaning at the intersection of lifeworlds and systemworlds.[16] However, imagination without the input of tradition fails to inculcate habits of conduct within students that preserve their sense of continuity with the past. Tradition refers to the customs and meanings around which a community unites as well as the transmission of these customs and

14. Carter, *Civility*.
15. Fluker, *Stones*.
16. Ibid.

ways of thinking to the next generation. The return to tradition, of course, as a repository of meaning and direction for present and future leadership has its inherent dangers. Any casual observation of the national and global conflicts surrounding religion, race, and ethnicity should sound a warning of the consequences of unreflective attachment to tradition. What I envision is more closely akin to what the great sociologist Edward Shils[17] had in mind when he referred to tradition. He suggests:

> Traditions are beliefs, standards and rules, of varying but never exhaustive explicitness, which have been received from the preceding generation through a process of continuous transmission from generation to generation. They recommend themselves by their appropriateness to the present situation confronted by their recipients and especially by a certain measure of authoritativeness that they possess by virtue of their provenience from the past. [The authority of tradition is not registered for its own sake or because] "it had always been that way" . . . Tradition is not the dead hand of the past, rather *the hand of the gardener* [italics added], which nourishes and elicits tendencies of judgment which would otherwise not be strong enough to emerge on their own.[18]

For instance, African American moral traditions have shaped ethical leaders who exhibit habits and practices that conspire against the unjust institutional practices that promote an unhealthy and self-destructive existence. Indeed, these leaders have worked in the cause of promoting institutional practices that support the health of the community. As Tavis Smiley notes in "Some Thoughts on Black Leadership," "All of the folk in our history that we respect and admire and uplift are the folk who found a way to serve."

As these traditions have played a significant role in shaping the moral languages of this nation, an operative assumption presented here is that retrieval and critical reframing of different cultural traditions and practices can serve both as strategic and instructive resources in the formation of ethical leaders for the twenty-first century.[19] At stake in the definition of ethical leadership that will be discussed is the larger discussion of what constitutes "ethical" and who determines what is "ethical leadership." As I write in *Ethical Leadership* (2009):

---

17. Shils, "Tradition and Liberty."
18. Grosby, *Virtue*, 106–7.
19. Fluker and Tumber, *Strange Freedom*.

Often, when we use terms like "ethical leadership," it is done without any critical or reflective thought. The words "ethical" and "leader" are so well entrenched in everyday speech that it is difficult to dislodge them from their popular, though largely unexamined, meanings. When most people think of ethical leadership, they tend to imbue leadership with values or a certain kind of moral character that we have witnessed in particular individuals. These associations are correct, but ethics and leadership are a lot like love and war—all is fair, but underneath their common employment lie a multitude of sins and methodological errors. For instance, "ethical" in certain contexts does not properly apply in others. Clearly, the moral quagmires of same-sex marriage, euthanasia, stem cell research and abortion are testaments of what is at stake for ethical questions raised in public life. Moral norms and customs that are so easily accepted within certain communities of discourse and practice run into complex conundrums when placed in a larger public debate where a diversity of views prevails.[20]

The Ethical Leadership Model® identifies the habits, practices, and excellencies for which moral human beings strive, and that ethical leaders must demonstrate in respect to self and others.

Finally, this paper will propose a framework that consists of the three aforementioned decisive nodal points for infusing culture and diversity into curricular strategies: *character* (personal), *civility* (social and public), and *community* (the larger spiritual nexus of communal belonging and practice). The outcomes of this approach are to empower students through storytelling (narrativization as a critical skill for remembering, retelling, and reliving their stories in the context of other cultural narratives); to provide resources for teaching skills and competencies for negotiation, tolerance, and appreciation of difference (looking, listening, and learning from the other's stories); and ethical decision making (discerning, deliberating, and deciding on appropriate conduct in relation to the other). In the interest of economy, these sets of competencies and skills will be integrated in the overall discussion that follows.

At the Intersection Where Worlds Collide

A favorite exercise that I use in workshops with emerging leaders in different cultures and traditions is to ask them to stand, close their eyes, and

20. Fluker, *Ethical Leadership*, ix.

imagine that they are at the center of a busy intersection with traffic coming from all directions. I ask them to imagine that there are no stoplights or traffic cops—just oncoming traffic. I also ask them to imagine the sounds at the intersection: running motors, screeching brakes, screams and shouts from people on the sidewalks and in cafes. I ask them to visualize the intersection: people of all kinds moving back and forth with the pulsating rhythm of urban life—the beggar sitting in the wheelchair outside a building, children holding their parents' hands, and the rushing traffic coming towards them from the front, the rear, the left, and the right.

Then I ask, "How do you feel?"

The responses normally are, I am afraid; I am confused; I am paralyzed.

"What will you do?"

I will run and dodge the traffic. I will tell the traffic to stop! I will cry for help! I will pray to God! I don't know what to do!

"Do you know which way is north? Do you even have time to figure out which way is north?"

Most do not know which way is north. Compasses of all sorts, material and moral, come in handy when you are on hiking trips or sailing through life, but they really are useless at the intersection where most of our students live, work, play, and survive.

Finally, I ask, "How will you negotiate this traffic at the intersection?" Very few have credible responses. How to negotiate the traffic at the intersection where worlds of difference collide and to analyze and interrogate complex internal and environmental issues; to interpret data that do not fit into convenient categories or principles; and to discern one's fitting decisions and actions are dimensions of the problem of diversity and culture.[21]

Private and Public Spheres of the Intersection

First and foremost, the intersection is fiercely private: it is personal and intimate. This place is not merely psychological or social but profoundly spiritual. In respect to the formation and role of leadership education, my concern is with spirituality as a basis for ethical orientation. In the form of a question, we ask, how might we prepare student leaders to recognize the need for spirituality in the development of habits and practices that nurture morally anchored character, transformative acts of civility, and a sense of

21. Gallien and Jackson, "Character Development"; Wren and Mendoza, "Cultural Identity."

community; and how might these habits and practices provide students with the resources and skills to live and function well in a world of difference?

The intersection is also public in the sense that it is the space where citizens meet and engage in meaningful discussion and action about values; and where they hold one another accountable for what they know and value. *Knowing* and *valuing* in conflicting cultural contexts raise epistemic and axiological questions that demand the construction of a common *lifeworld*.[22] According to Augusto Blasi, "It is the task of psychology to find explanations for individual differences in the ways *understanding* and *motivation* [italics added] are related to each other and in the degree of congruence between these two elements of personality."[23] In the public sphere, issues such as class, gender, sexual orientation, race, ethnicity, and religion both form and inform the relationship between understanding and motivation in student behavior. Yet, the private self must have a public connection. That is, through a web of relationships and networks, students learn certain values and social determinants of behavior. The intersection represents, therefore, both private and public spaces where a new generation of student leadership must stand, negotiate, and redirect the traffic of lifeworlds and systemworlds.

Lifeworlds and Systemworlds

"Lifeworlds" refers to the commonplace, everyday traffic of life where people meet and greet one another, where common values and presuppositions about order and the world are held. "Systemworlds" refers to the vast, often impersonal bureaucratic systems dominated by money and power (economics and politics and the various structures of communications and technology), which are frequently at odds with the pedestrian traffic of lifeworlds. Lifeworlds are built upon social practices, traditions, and institutions that are often at odds with systemworlds, where technical reason and the relentless quest for power and money assault their very fragile existence. Students, whom educators encounter and serve in classrooms and other educational environments, are at these intersections often without the requisite skills and competencies needed not only to *tolerate* the other, but to *appreciate* the place of diversity and culture in their own lives and in

---

22. McCollough, *Moral Imagingation*.
23. Blasi, "Moral Character," 341.

the lives of others.[24] The development of leaders in this century will depend largely on the skill with which new generations of ethical leaders negotiate the traffic at these intersections, and on their ability to inspire and guide others to create community.

The Quest for Character and the Development of Ethical Student Leadership

The quest for character is a significant element in the ongoing debate on education, religion, and politics in American society and has significant implications for the development of students and, by implication, educators in a post-American world.[25] The emphasis on character education as a means of meeting the complex challenges that the nation faces has been at the center of social reform promulgated by political and religious activism.[26] According to Cunningham,[27] the new character education movement that began in the 1990s bears striking parallels to the character education movements of the 1910s and the 1920s and all are synonymous with "school improvement." The upsurge in religious activism in the quest for character education reflects the larger issue of ideology and values inherited from a mechanistic model that places emphasis on fixing and adjusting things. These crusades represent dangerous signs in our culture; in our political, civic, and religious institutions; and in our schools.[28]

In the following, I am interested in character as an adventure of sorts, a quest for the unity of self and consciousness; more like a prize or a goal that is sought, which is akin to the Platonic tradition that honors *anamnesis* and has implications for our later discussion on remembering, retelling, and reliving stories.[29] As we shall see, it is a narrative quest for unity in the context of larger social-historical narratives. For diverse and marginalized students, the problem of character education is most urgent because it addresses the very complex issues of identity, purpose, and meaning not

---

24. Wren and Mendoza, "Cultural Identity."
25. Zakaria, *The Post-American World*.
26. Cochran-Smith, *Walking the Road*; Scapp, *Teaching Values*.
27. Cunningham, "Certain and Reasoned Art."
28. Cornwall, "The Problem with Character Education"; Fogel, *Fourth Great Awakening*; Nash, "Post-Modern Reflection."
29. Hauerwas, *Community of Character*; MacIntyre, *After Virtue*; Wren, "Philosophical Moorings."

simply in personal and existential terms, but in respect to relation, which is simultaneously social and public. For educators this will require the development of innovative and imaginative curricular strategies, pedagogies, and practices that address the questions of diversity, globalization, and change; and courageous institutional leadership and support.[30] The following section addresses these questions through a framework that incorporates a curricular strategy utilizing character, civility, and community as primary sites of student moral development and leadership.

I describe ethical leadership as the critical appropriation and embodiment of moral traditions that have shaped the character and shared meanings of a people (an ethos). In fact, ethical leadership does not emerge from an historical vacuum but arises from the lifeworlds of particular traditions and speaks authoritatively and acts responsibly with the aim of serving the collective good. Ethical leaders, therefore, are leaders whose characters have been shaped by the wisdom, habits, and practices of particular traditions, often more than one, yet they tend to be identified with a specific cultural ethos and narrative. Finally, ethical leadership asks the question of values in reference to ultimate concern.[31] Ethical student leadership as described here will receive elaboration in the discussion that follows.

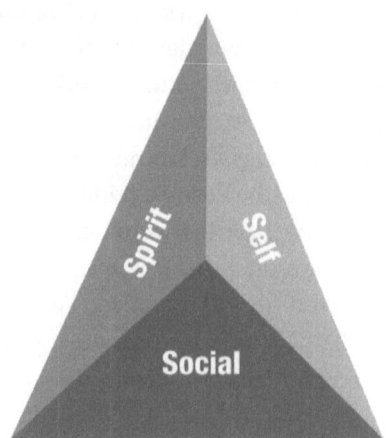

Figure 1.1. Ethical Leadership™ Self, Social, and Spiritual

This understanding of ethical leadership is based upon a triangular model that incorporates three dynamically interrelated dimensions of

30. Anderson, *Driving Change*; Zakaria, *The Post-American World*.
31. Fluker, *Stones*.

human existence: *self, social,* and *spiritual.* In the dimension of the *self* or the personal, the concern is with questions of identity and purpose: Who am I? What do I want? What do I propose to do and to become? The *social* or public dimension involves the relationship with the other and leads one to ask: To whom and to what am I ultimately accountable? Last, the *spiritual* dimension addresses the human need for a sense of ultimacy, excellence, and hope in reference to the great mystery of being. In addition to the questions posed by self, it also asks: Who is the other? How am I to respond to the actions of the other towards me? As stated, this latter dimension should not be narrowly identified with religion, although religious experience can be a vital resource in one's spiritual quest. For this third dimension, I am more interested in answering questions of identity and purpose as they relate to leaders' perceptions of their own search for meaning in relation to the demands of the other, which raises basic questions of recognition, respect, and reverence; and of courage, justice, and compassion.

Character and Ethical Leadership

Following the triadic framework outlined above, the model addresses the psychological, social, and spiritual dimensions of ethical leadership in respect to character, civility, and a sense of community. Within each dimension of character, civility, and community, there are attendant *virtues* (good habits that aspire to cognitive competency and emotional sensibility), *values* (good habits that drive social practices in public space), and *virtuosities* (the excellencies of a virtuous life that drive behavior at personal and public levels). Ethical leaders come into being through the development of character, civility, and a sense of community. This triune of virtues, values, and virtuosities is the bedrock for genuine human development, productivity, and peaceful co-existence.

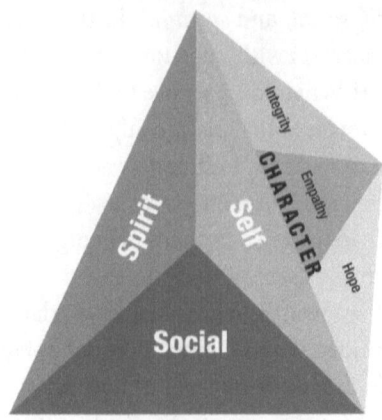

Figure 1.2. Ethical Leadership™ The Defining Virtues of Character

Character as Narrative Quest

The notion of character, as the personal dimension of leadership, refers to the narrative script that defines the individual; the stories that name the student's experience; and the "inner experience" or core philosophies espoused by the individual. Character is understood as comprehensively including *thinking, feeling,* and *behavior*.[32] The cultivation of the private life or the student's inner theater is the basis for spirituality and ethical awareness. Leaders involved in acts of personal and social transformation must begin by remembering, retelling, and reliving their own stories. Character, in this sense, refers to "the morally anchored self in the context of socio-historical narrative." For our purposes, this means that student leaders must examine their life experiences in relation to larger historical and cultural narratives. Reclaiming the ethical center requires that the unfinished business of the student's life story (the pains, the hurts, the unresolved contradictions) be addressed. It also means reattachment to historically grounded values that have protected their communities through ritualistic healing, bringing about integrity and self-esteem, trust and empathy, courage and hope as personal and social practices. Howard Gardner's definition of a leader is helpful in this regard in that he emphasizes the tripartite construction of cognition, affection, and behavior. "A leader is an individual (or, rarely, a

---

32. Lickona et al., "CEP's Eleven Principles."

set of individuals) who significantly affects the thoughts, feelings, and/or behaviors of a significant number of individuals."[33]

Defining Virtues of Character

Attendant to character, student leaders should allow three virtues to become part and parcel of their focus and personal deportment. They are, respectively, *integrity, empathy,* and *hope*. In the tradition of Aristotle, I define *virtues* as "good habits" or as an "organized set of habits of reaction."[34]

Integrity

Integrity refers to a sense of wholeness, a sense of community within self: in sum, what Howard Thurman called *a healthy sense of self*.[35] A threefold process (identity, purpose, and method) begins with the development of a healthy sense of self, which is the basis upon which one comes to understand one's own distinctive potential and self-worth, without which students drift aimlessly through life without a true understanding of their place in existence. This is an especially significant issue for students from marginalized groups who have been misnamed by a culture in often subtle and surreptitious ways. Integrity informs the student leader's actions and practices and has a definitive impact on how he or she responds to the other with sincerity and truthfulness.[36] It is also the key unifying virtue in the student's response to dehumanizing actions and other forces that work against human development and community. This idea of integrity, as a good habit that is practiced, is pivotal in negotiating incoherent frames of reference at the intersection of complex diverse cultural situations. As Wren and Mendoza claim, the bicultural subjects of their study "demonstrated that [the subjects'] competencies . . . are the enhanced abilities to negotiate differences and disjunctures with hopes of ameliorating their complexities." Without integrity, students are unable to negotiate "acceptance of internal conflicts, dichotomous self-images, competing group loyalties, and other sorts of fluidity and ambiguity."[37]

---

33. Gardner, *Leading Minds*, ix; Shusterman, "Somaesthetics."
34. James, *Talks to Teachers*, 184; Pawelski, "Pragmatism."
35. Fluker, *They Looked for a City*; Thurman, *Deep Is the Hunger*, 64, 93.
36. Carter, *Integrity*; Dreher, *Tao of Personal Leadership*.
37. Wren and Mendoza, "Cultural Identity," 254–56.

Empathy

Related to integrity is *empathy*, the psychosocial dimension of character. For our purposes, empathy is the capacity of the ethical leader to put himself or herself in the other's place. It is correlated with *respect of the other* and thrives best where there are shared visions and goals. Empathy is really about feelings—intelligent feelings that have been cultivated through practice.[38] Empathy, in this sense, is a "lower order virtue" that is connected to respect and justice, as correlates in the development of public and social interactions.[39]

The practice of empathy for others creates a moral ethos within communities of discourse and practice. For student leaders, communities of discourse and practice refer to the contexts of their primary social relations with other students, educators, and the larger public where they are called upon to continually negotiate difference. Imagination plays an important role in this process. Through the use of imagination, students are enabled to transcend self and to empathize with others at the seat of "common consciousness." In doing so, others are addressed at a place beyond all blame and fault—and *difference*. Integral to the practice of empathy is the ability of learning to listen to the other's story without *incorporation* or *indifference*. Learning to listen involves sounding the other out, self-regulating, waiting, and responding to the other, however different, with genuineness and integrity.

Hope

I define *hope* as genuine anticipation of the future. Genuine anticipation of the future is rooted in the confidence that the future is open, and that new possibilities of life exist. Marianne Williamson's edited volume, *Imagine What America Could Be in the 21st Century*,[40] is a great example of what is at stake for students and educators across various disciplines and domains who dare to use imagination as a tool for envisioning possibility. One of the articles, written by Peter Senge,[41] suggests that imagining new futures allows us to see possibility beyond the fixed patterns of the Machine System, which has been the dominant paradigm since the Industrial Age. He suggests three ways of thinking about the future: (1) to conceive of the future as an extension of the past (extrapolation); (2) to imagine what might be, independent

---

38. Goleman, et al., *Primal Leadership*.
39. Blasi, "Moral Character."
40. Williamson, *Imagine What America Could Be*.
41. Senge, "Systems."

of what is, or as free of the influence of the present as one might become; and (3) to cultivate awareness and reflectiveness—to become open to what is arising in the world and in us, and to continually ponder what matters most deeply to us. The third option, he thinks, is the way of the future and requires creative use of the imagination. For leadership education, *awareness* and *effectiveness*, or heart and head, are both integral to the practice of imagining. The cognitive faculty is not in alien territory in imaginative adventures, as is often thought; rather it is a key asset.[42] Anne Colby argues that hope and inspiration may very well be the missing links in empowering disaffected and disempowered groups to become more engaged in the political processes that determine our corporate destiny as citizens.

> But we know from American and world history that ordinary people, including members of disempowered groups, can make a difference politically if they work together and believe there is some hope for change. Offering that hope and galvanizing collective action around those goals is the essence of leadership, and we know that people can be transformed by inspiring leaders, coming to believe that they can make a difference. The question for higher education is how to foster in students a sense that individuals' civic and political actions matter.[43]

Colby's call for hope and inspiration demands intelligent, pragmatic, and concrete proposals for action and implementation of a vertically integrated system of diversity and globalization that "expects accountability and rewards commitment to change."[44] The quest for civility takes this sense of accountability and commitment to change as a critical step in the development of an infusion strategy for diversity and culture.

Civility and Ethical Leadership

The Quest for Civility

Civility is used in a variety of contexts, often masking complex historical, sociological, and methodological issues. In common usage, *civility* refers to a set of manners—certain etiquettes and social graces rooted in specific class orientations and moral sensibilities, which is the way most character

42. Ayers, *Teaching the Personal*.
43. Colby, "Fostering the Moral," 407.
44. Anderson, *Driving Change*, 41.

education initiatives and programs use it as well. *Civility*, however, does not refer simply to etiquette, manners, and social graces, but it includes social capital and the inherent benefits accrued by these networks of reciprocity. This is an important distinction for the development of civility among students. Civility also has to do with the student's social dignity within systems. It represents the public space of the student where she negotiates the intersection between lifeworlds and systemworlds. The power of market-stimulated moralities and the waning interest in civic life forecast an ominous future for American democracy, especially for many students who have been marginalized at the boundaries of a social contract that from its inception was exclusive and xenophobic.[45] Beyond the impact of various forms of media on the prosocial behavior of students and adults is the persistent and inadequately documented effect on the question of diversity and the cultural designation of the other as the hostile stranger.

In our model, the term *civility* is used as a framework for understanding the role of social capital within the context of students' social and public life practices. I do not limit *civility*, however, to social capital, but refer more broadly to the concept as the social-historical script or contract that the student citizen negotiates within the context of the larger society. Civility is the psychosocial ecology of the student: a certain understanding or self-referential index of the student's place within a social system as it relates to personal character. This description of social capital and its role in creating and sustaining community is important for the ethical student's moral development in two ways. First, social capital provides networks for community engagement that can be inclusive and socially beneficial for the student and his or her environment; and second, social capital derives its life and power from the norms of reciprocity that it engenders and sustains. Ethical leadership in the classroom or on the playground is essential for the maintenance of social capital. Moreover, civility is the fuel of a strong democratic culture that ensures opportunity and stability for future leaders. Civility, therefore, protects and promotes the key values of liberty, equality, and friendship, without which democracy is impossible, and which emerging leaders must learn and practice. One may not think of *friendship* as a value that must be learned and practiced, but as Preston King points out, friendship is (regrettably) not a factor in contemporary public discourse. In "The Decline of Friendship in Modernity: Issues and Challenges for Ethical Leadership," which follows later on in this volume, King asserts: "In

---

45. Fluker, "Recognition."

conditions of modernity, friendship has long been in decline. On balance, this probably can have a debilitating impact on the quality of contemporary life, and on the question of leadership."[46]

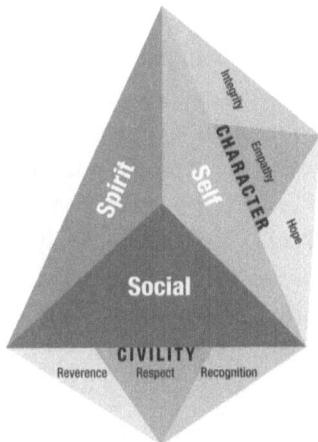

Figure 1.3. Ethical Leadership™ Defining Virtues and Values

Following our model, there are three interrelated values of civility: *recognition* (personal), *respect* (public), and *reverence* (spirit). In each dimension of civility, as we shall see, there is also the circular movement from *personal* to *public* to *spirit*.

Defining Values of Civility

Recognition

Recognition in ethical leadership practices begins with consciousness, a focused awareness that is extended through the self and through others, and to ultimate frames of references. First, recognition as an activity of consciousness has neither moral nor ethical significance. It insists, rather, on the development of a sense of transcendence in which one is able to self-observe as one observes others. This mode of consciousness is sometimes called *self-awareness* or *self-observation*. Self-observation allows the student to become aware or to recognize herself and to better understand the unconscious motivations that drive thoughts, feelings, and behavior. For student leaders' moral and social development, this focused awareness of the

46. See below, p. 104.

self is of paramount importance. The significance of self-observation for civility lies first in the students' personal quests for self-dignity and respect. It also serves as a major fount for the quest of remembering their story and how that story is intertwined with the stories of others. No greater work can be done by the student in repairing the ethical center than becoming aware of his or her inherent worth and dignity, especially when confronted with judgment, blame, and mistrust that arise in diverse cultural situations. As a practical consideration in promoting healthy environments of diversity, the aim is to create networks of reciprocity and social capital that are based on trust. Beyond social contracting in the formal sense of legislating and mandating institutional codes and values, civility rests on covenantal relations that require integrity, empathy, and hope, which engender and sustain friendship. Friendship extends beyond utility and duty and rests ultimately upon common purpose and vision.[47]

Respect

Respect is the public analogue of civility and has profound implications for citizenship. In the perspective of civility I am proposing, respect has to do with the accepted standards of association of free people (citizens) and with social dignity. In this view, respect includes: (1) a certain self-referential index that recognizes oneself as inhering and therefore deserving certain acknowledgements of one's human dignity in public space; and (2) a responsibility to demonstrate in public space one's obligation to the other as inhering and therefore deserving certain acknowledgements of human dignity. Fundamental to this twofold definition of *respect* is the relation between empathy and balance. In this view, Sara Lawrence-Lightfoot's excellent and creative exploration of respect as a nonhierarchal expression of human relationship is invaluable for the task of developing ethical student leadership.[48] Lawrence-Lightfoot notes that respect is often viewed as "a debt due people because of their attained or inherited position, age, gender, class, race, professional status, accomplishments, etc. Whether defined by rules of law, habits or culture, respect often implies required expressions of esteem, approbation, or submission." By contrast, her "focus is on the way respect creates symmetry, empathy, and connection in all kinds of relationships,"[49]

47. King and Devere, *The Challenge to Friendship*.
48. Lawrence-Lightfoot, *Respect*.
49. Ibid., 9–10.

which allows students to move beyond strictly hierarchal, rules-based management perspectives, but aspires to the cultivation of a *moral ethos* that creates balance, creativity, and imaginative enterprise with others.

Reverence

Reverence is a tricky term in the context of leadership education. I am using *reverence* in much the same sense as I use *spiritual*. Fundamentally, reverence concerns recognition and respect of the other and their keen interrelatedness to one's self. *Reverence* is preceded by *loyalty*. One of the supreme tests of civility has been and continues to be the question of loyalty. For instance, loyalty to friends, groups, and traditions can create serious ethical dilemmas for students in respect to diversity and inclusiveness. The dilemma for students is how to reconcile competing demands for loyalty: the inclusive demand of one's own moral vision versus the often contradicting demands of friendship, belonging, ideology, race, ethnicity, sexuality, and religious beliefs. Loyalty is not easily defined. It is one of those elusive terms like *love* because it is attached to something profoundly spiritual. Loyalty in its most fundamental sense is a discipline of informed consent of the will to a higher cause to which the person seeks union within the self and with others. But loyalty, for the ethical student leader, does not seek confirmation from external events or rewards, but finds its genesis and actualization in the integrity of the cause to which the leader is committed. The spiritual unity that loyalty seeks finds its fullest expression in reverence for life. Ethical student leaders should not, therefore, allow their loyalties to kin, group, nation, or even religious beliefs to supersede the ethic of reverence for life.[50] Reverence for life appeals to something that is fundamentally human that seeks ultimate unity found in a *sense of community*.[51]

Community and Ethical Leadership

The Quest for Community

The quest for community, like the quests for character and civility, has a long and ambivalent history in American society and has significant implications for the issues of diversity and culture in leadership education.

---

50. Clark, *Ethical Mysticism*; Schweitzer, "Ethics of Reverence."
51. Capra, *Web of Life*; Devall and Sessions, *Deep Ecology*.

Since its founding, the nation has struggled with the antagonistic twins of self-reliance and community. The American obsession with self-reliance, liberty, and individualism has created another dynamic that undermines the country's moral vision of community and challenges the task of creating diversity. A point of departure is the moral language of community, which arises from the traditions, institutions, and social practices of civility that have historically nurtured and sustained our democracy but with important twists. Such a departure involves a community of memory, but not necessarily the communities of memory that have been the dominant voices in the making of America.[52] The memories of John Winthrop's "City on a Hill," Thomas Jefferson's "Notes on the State of Virginia," or Walt Whitman's "I Sing America" will not suffice for a fuller and more accurate retelling of the American story for our nation's students.

Many of our students come from places on the periphery with distinctive perspectives that dare to see kaleidoscopic visions of America's future in a world where difference and the jagged edges of history collide at the intersection. We are continually discovering that traditional understandings of character and civility without a diverse community of memory that informs ethical orientation are bereft of authority and influence in our classrooms. Questions of the good, beautiful, and just are spinning at astronomical speeds in our culture, and there is great anxiety about lost values and the need to return to the past for direction. Amid religiously inspired debates about values and political jostling on leveraging advantage, Americans are asking themselves which way is north, but this is a highly relative question. For those who stand at different places with very different stories, one's "north" may be another's "south."

Kwame Anthony Appiah has suggested that the future of cosmopolitanism hinges on how well we distinguish between *thin* and *thick* moral arguments in public debates, and that in the final analysis, learning to live with different interpretations of values relies more on *practice* than on argumentation.[53] The emphasis ought to be on listening to the other, which is a disciplined practice that involves personal virtues (integrity, empathy, and hope) that are related to character and to analogous public values (recognition, respect, and reverence), which form the basis of civility and a sense of community. In fact the ground has shifted with respect to the question of traditional morals and values and how they inform direction at

---

52. Morris and Weaver, *Difficult Memories*; Spalding et al., "March of Remembrance."
53. Appiah, *Cosmopolitanism*.

the intersection. This fact alone challenges some of the very basic presuppositions of character and leadership education in America.

Most student development models that use leadership education as a resource and strategy point toward the individual student as the source and director of the moral compass, with an emphasis on the classical Western tradition as the narrative repository of virtue. One of the challenges that educators in the US will increasingly face will be how to accommodate students from places that were not a part of the original blueprint. The contemporary debate on immigration policies provides a sobering look at the deep and abiding fissures that plague narrow and myopic visions of citizenship. Immigration is more than an issue of what constitutes citizenship and entitlement in our democracy. It is an issue about who will lead—and by virtue of this question, who gets educated and how they get educated. In the late 1950s, John F. Kennedy wrote in *A Nation of Immigrants*: "Immigration policy should be generous; it should be fair; it should be flexible . . . With such a policy, we can turn to the world and to our own past with clean hands and a clear conscience . . . The immigrants we welcome today and tomorrow will carry on this tradition and help us to retain, reinvigorate and strengthen the American spirit."[54]

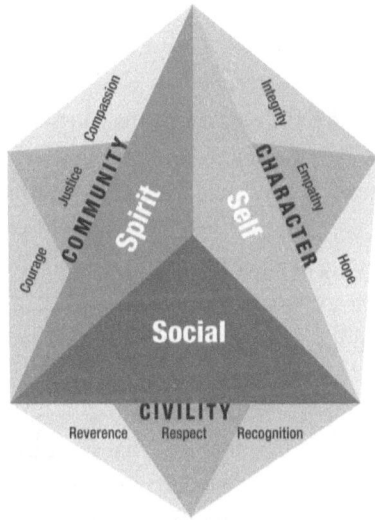

Figure 1.4. Ethical Leadership™ Defining Virtues, Values, and Virtuosities of Character, Civility, and Community

---

54. Kennedy, *A Nation of Immigrants*, 53.

Educating Leaders for the Twenty-First Century

A Sense of Community

A sense of community represents the spiritual dimension in the tripartite model of ethical leadership. Community as a rational construction is the ideal that serves as the goal of human existence and the norm for ethical judgment. Concretely expressed, it is the mutually cooperative and voluntary venture of persons in which they realize the solidarity of humanity by freely assuming responsibility for one another within the context of civil relations. Leadership education, therefore, must begin with community as both the source and the end of all practices associated with the development of leaders. As we have discussed, integrity (as a sense of wholeness, integration, and balance) is the work of community within self. One can hardly hope to create community in the world without first looking deeply within the self and discovering the challenges of creating a healthy sense of self. Furthermore, community provides the context for the sensuous articulation of the values of compassion, justice, and courage as dynamic and interrelated practices. *Community* refers to a sense of unity and interdependence with nature as a whole; the centrality of civil society in the development of self-worth and affirmation; community occurring as a network of extended families; and other institutions as media through which persons share their sense of self and belonging: a common ground upon which the diversity of people and/or ideas and values can unite in a spiritual reality marked by appreciation of difference.[55]

In "The Role of Ethical Behavior in the Elimination of Disparities in Health," David Satcher writes about an issue that cries out for a solution based on *a sense of community*. That issue is the existence of disparities in health in the US. It is becoming increasingly urgent that leaders address the healthcare crisis from the perspective of *community*, from a frame of reference that takes as its starting point the imperative that to be *in community* is to assume responsibility for one another and to recognize the inherent worth of each person regardless of our differences. Satcher describes disparities in health among different racial groups—such as mortality rates from diabetes and cancer—and lays out what we must do as a community to eliminate such disparities. He argues that we need ethical leaders who will work to change the social determinants of health—the conditions in which people are born, learn, grow, work, and age. Satcher notes that we need ethical leaders who possess individual integrity (character), who treat

---

55. Fluker, *They Looked for a City*.

others with respect (civility), and who think of others, not only of themselves, when making decisions and setting policies regarding healthcare and health insurance mandates (community).

The significance of community for self and civil society is the primary concern of our model for the development of ethical leadership. A healthy sense of self is intricately related to the interaction between self and society. In respect to this interactive model of self and society, the quest for personal identity (for understanding and motivation) is inextricably bound to the quest for wholeness, harmony, and integration in society. Our model seeks to engage students in the quest for community at personal and social levels through the production of their own rituals or creative exercises. For ethical student leaders, the primary questions are: How do we create and maintain a responsible and respectful relationship with each other in the quest for community, and how does this model relate to the broader and critical issues of ethical student leadership that have been already discussed? Three attendant practices or virtuosities (i.e., personal and social quests for courage, justice, and compassion) define community.

Defining Virtuosities of Community

Courage

Almost every ancient philosopher considers *courage* to be a virtue. It is no accident that the ancients located courage around the heart. Courage is a balanced coordination of both the mind (cognition) and the will (volition). While courage has a rational component, as Aristotle pointed out, it requires more than knowledge; it has rather to do with achieving balance between extremes of foolhardiness and fear. For instance, in particular contexts of diversity, "the virtue of courage may be specifically targeted in an IEP [individualized educational program] for a student with a disability who must learn to be a self-advocate, to assure that his or her rights are not restricted."[56] Leadership education must include nontraditional strategies that teach students to balance these extremes through practice.

Justice

Justice refers to the social and public spheres with which students engage, but it begins with *a sense of justice*. Human beings, especially children,

---

56. Lehr, et al., "Character Education," 77.

display what James Q. Wilson calls "the moral sense," certain natural sensibilities "formed out of the interaction of their innate dispositions with their earliest familial experiences . . . That moral sense shapes human behavior and the judgments people make of the behavior of others."[57] The moral sense of justice, according to Wilson, precedes social constructs of justice as in rules, principles, and laws, yet it informs how certain rational renderings of justice are shaped by traditions and customs of different cultures. Each person "struggles to reconcile the partially warring parts of his universally occurring nature—the desire for survival and sustenance with the desire for companionship and approval,"[58] and is constantly in pursuit of social arrangements that best provide for these basic needs and desires. A sense of justice as fairness arises from this basic human instinct. It has its genesis in early childhood associations with family and kin and is expressed in feelings of equity, reciprocity, and impartiality.

Harvard law professor Lani Guinier tells the story of a discussion that she had with her four-year-old son, Nikolas, about a *Sesame Street Magazine* exercise.[59] The exercise pictured six children, four with hands raised, indicating their choice to play tag; and two whose hands were down because they wanted to play hide-and-seek. The magazine asked the readers to count the number of children who wanted to play tag and the number who wanted to play hide-and-seek, and to decide which game the children would play. To his mother's surprise, Nikolas responded, "They will play both. First they will play tag. Then they will play hide-and-seek." Despite the rules implied by the exercise, Guinier says Nikolas was right. It is natural for children to take turns. "The winner may get to play first or more often, but even the 'loser' gets something."[60] Nikolas's wisdom underscores a fundamental issue at stake in respect to justice as fairness. The prevalent practice of "winners take all" flies in the face of the idea of community that we are espousing. But in political elections and corporate takeovers, and in the game of nations, this is the norm. Students learn early that in a world of winners and losers, there is little room for principles of equity, reciprocity, and impartiality; and they act it out in classrooms and in the larger environment. The idea of winners taking all also circumvents the project of democracy as embracing difference and inclusion. Losers are the minority and are forever disadvantaged,

57. Wilson, *Moral Sense*, 2.
58. Ibid., 122–23.
59. Guinier, *Tyranny of the Majority*.
60. Ibid., 2.

suggests Guinier, by "the tyranny of the majority." Rather than a zero-sum game where winners take all, leadership education should seek *positive sum solutions* "in which all perspectives are represented and in which all people work together to find common ground."[61]

Compassion

The third and most important dimension of the ethical student leader's practice that anticipates community is compassion. Compassion is the supreme virtuosity of ethical leadership. Within our proposed framework, compassion is located on the spiritual side of the triangle and is the culmination of hope and reverence—and indeed of all the practices. The model begins with integrity and ends in compassion. Compassion is the fulfillment of the *virtues* of character: integrity, empathy, and hope; it provides the moral fabric for the *values* of civility: recognition, respect, and reverence; and the *virtuosities* of courage and justice find their fulfillment in acts of compassion.

Conclusion and Recommendations

In summary, the challenge of the infusion of diversity and culture in leadership education requires the development of innovative and imaginative curricular strategies, pedagogies, and practices that address the questions of diversity, globalization, and change; and courageous institutional leadership and support. The framework discussed in this paper has attempted to do so by placing methodological emphasis on the nodal concepts of character, civility, and community. Outlined below are more concrete strategies that can be customized to address students, teachers, administrators, corporations, nonprofit organizations, and human resource departments, along with specific communities of discourse and practices in variable educational situations.

Storytelling and Rituals

Telling stories has long been recognized as an important part of healing, self-knowledge, and personal and spiritual development. Stories make claims on our minds and hearts often before we know why or how. We

---

61. Guinier, *Tyranny of the Majority*, 6.

are drawn into a tale without permission, forethought, or desire to be involved.[62] The types of stories with which this approach is concerned are parabolic and mythical.

Parables are stories that highlight and create contradiction in order to reveal a truth otherwise hidden. Parabolic stories introduce contradiction into situations of complacent security and invite transformation by opening students to the possibility of something new. On the other hand, *myth* mediates between two irreducible opposites and seeks to resolve the contradiction and paradox; myths presume the possibility of such reconciliation.[63] As students are drawn into these stories, the customs, ways of thinking, and creative resolutions utilized by story characters will be transmitted to others towards the end of creating diverse understandings of others and forming community. The stories and myths can cover a wide range, including classical philosophical and literary traditions, history, current events, and ancient folklore from different traditions.

Rituals are solemn rites and routines, repetition of rigorously enforced sensuous acts in the internalization of virtues, values, and virtuosities. Rituals that are appropriate to the story being told should be utilized. Students must be given opportunities to apply their new insights to their own parables and myths. For instance, in the retelling of Plato's Allegory of the Cave, students can be assigned the task of creating an accompanying ritual to provide sensuous articulation to the dominant themes of the story (bondage of consciousness; enlightenment and liberation, integrity, empathy, hope and respect for the other, and so on).

Aesthetic Triggers

In addition to story and ritual, immersion in aesthetic or artistic enterprise is a powerful stimulus to imagining alternatives. After participating in an act of artistic creation, students view the world differently. They see the world as malleable and open to difference, which triggers consciousness of difference that can be utilized as a learning resource for diversity. Examples of aesthetic triggers are origami, mask-making, tai chi, dance,

---

62. Nash, *Liberating Scholarly Writing*.

63. Assmann, *Moses the Egyptian*; Levi-Strauss, *Structural Anthropology*; Ricoeur, *Symbolism of Evil*.

community banner-making, spoken word, poetry, fantasy, drawing, photography, painting, songwriting, and drama.[64]

Poetry

Through poetic formats and conventions, students are given permission to externalize their most private feelings. In a poem, students can give voice to their wildest imaginings without fear of being criticized for their lack of rationale. Writing a poem or a letter positively reinforces forms of imaginative speculation that students would be too embarrassed to admit to in other, more "rational" contexts.[65]

Writing

Writing compositions or short episodes of fantasy can be extremely liberating.[66] These fantasies may be exercised in a straightforward projective speculation; for example, "If you were an immigrant from _____, how would you feel and what would you do to change relations in this classroom, school, community, nation, and the world?"; or they may be less focused. Sometimes giving students a single, powerful word (for example, *gay*) and asking them to put that feeling or state of being into words can be a highly provocative exercise.

Art

Students who feel uncomfortable writing private fantasies can be encouraged to depict their fantasies visually in paintings, drawings, photography, or audio-visual media such as voice recordings on CD or mp3. Once the teacher has assured students that the exercise is not a test of their artistic abilities, their imaginations are freed to explore possibilities that are new, open, and inclusive.

Vocalization

Community singing has long been used as a means of building some sense of group cohesion. The imaginative power and creative skill depicted in Hip Hop is a prime example. Through poetry, music, and song, slaves

---

64. Rosaen, "Preparing Teachers"; Tisdell, "In the New Millennium."
65. Tisdell, "In the New Millennium."
66. Lunsford and Ouzgane, *Crossing Borderlands*.

expressed and preserved their humanity. These songs literally acted as a form of resistance to the oppressive forces working upon them. Spoken word exercises and songwriting are also important techniques for building solidarity among students and for empowering them to transcend assumptions, beliefs, and biases against others.

Drama

To dramatize commonly occurring, shared situations of diversity and difference, and how these might be acted upon, is a powerful way of releasing imaginative speculation. Improvisational theater can be very effective in dramatizing common problems, concerns, and experiences relating to diversity and culture. Role-playing not only helps individuals take the perspective of others but also brings to their consciousness some of the feelings and emotions that inform the thoughts and actions of others.

Play

Last, experiential learning games are useful supplements to strengthen diversity in learning. Extensive presentations of concepts, theories, and models will bore almost any audience. Games can provide vivid examples that will be implanted in students' memories for longer periods of time.

Debriefing, Analysis, and Reflection

Crucial to all these aesthetic triggers is some form of debriefing, analysis, and reflection. Debriefing by a trained educator supplemented by journalizing is an essential element of this approach. It is important that the students, as the creators of fantasies, songs, photographs, etc., be encouraged to reflect on the forces that inspired these activities and how they are related to character, civility, and community. After imagining in fictional or dramatized form how their situations appear to others, and after hearing how others respond to these, students may find it easier to conceive of alternative ways of discerning, deliberating, and acting within diverse situations. If they have been able to imagine alternatives in poetry, fantasy, art, and drama, it will be more possible for them to imagine alternatives in their own real lives and in the treatment of others who are different. By helping students recognize how their powers of imagination have been engaged, they will begin to realize that they possess creative, speculative capacities and that they can call on these for a variety of purposes. Once the capacity to imagine alternatives in aesthetic domains has been realized, it is but a short step to considering how this activity might be replicated in relationships with others and systems.

Critical Thinking

Though critical thinking is a key skill for students, it is not often thought to use critical thinking as a preventive tool for individuals living at the nexus of complex and conflicting pressures. However, the imaginative skills that underlie critical thinking are needed by "at risk" students living at the nexus of lifeworlds and systems who must negotiate public space with others.

Without these skills, students will fail to develop: (1) confidence about their potential for changing aspects of their diverse worlds as individuals and in collective action; (2) an appreciation for diversity, creativity, innovation, and a life full of possibilities; (3) an understanding of the future as malleable, not closed and fixed; and (4) the agency to create and re-create aspects of their personal, social, and spiritual lives in pursuit of a world of diversity and change.

Critical thinking is a natural outgrowth of the healing work of story, ritual, and aesthetic triggers upon the ethical centers of students as it is the skill of imaginative speculation that produces and sustains the critical thinker. Exercises in critical thinking can serve as an appropriate vehicle for the enhancement and internalization of students' newly acquired imaginative skills. The three forms of critical thinking with which the proposed framework is concerned are: (1) reflective learning or reframing, (2) dialectical thinking, and (3) emancipatory learning.

Reflective Learning or Reframing

Reflective learning is the process of internally examining and exploring an issue of concern as in diversity and culture, triggered by an experience, which creates and clarifies meaning in terms of self, and which results in a changed conceptual perspective. The outcome of reflective learning is a change in assumption about oneself and the world requiring a corresponding change in one's behavior and relationships.

Dialectical or Nondualistic Thinking

Dialectical thinking focuses on the understanding and resolution of contradictions. Dialectical thinking is thinking that looks for, recognizes, and welcomes contradictions (the other as stranger) as a stimulus for moral development.

Emancipatory Learning

Last, in emancipatory learning, students become aware of the forces that have brought them to their current situation and are empowered to take actions to change some aspect of these situations. In the case of diversity, it is important that students look to, listen, and learn from the other. Emancipatory learning frees students from personal, institutional, and environmental forces that prevent them from seeing new directions; being tolerant, respectful, and appreciative of difference; gaining control over aspects of their lives that appear different and strange to others; and working for transformation of their society and their world.

As can be seen, story, ritual, and the aesthetic triggers serve to spark the imaginative speculation skills that underlie these three forms of critical thinking. These aesthetic triggers not only serve to bring healing of and restoration of hope to the ethical centers of students, but they also facilitate the creation of critical thinkers, who call into question the assumptions underlying their habitual ways of thinking and acting that promote intolerance, violence, and disrespect; and examine them for accuracy and validity—ready to think and act differently on the basis of this critical questioning.

In summary, the methodological emphases of the proposed framework can serve as a critical resource and infusion strategy that:

- transmits through storytelling the customs and ways of thinking that promote the development of the personal constructs of an ethical center: character, civility, and community;
- utilizes ritual and other aesthetic triggers to help students interrogate and critique customs and ways of thinking that promote bigotry and xenophobia;
- utilizes critical thinking exercises to help students internalize imaginative skills needed to produce and sustain reflective learning, dialectic thinking, and emancipatory learning;

- facilitates their application of these skills to solve lifeworld and system problems that promote and sustain intolerance, violence, and disrespect for the other;

- provides students with an experience of community through which the natural development of ethical judgment in favor of tolerance, appreciation, and acceptance of difference is stimulated; and

- provides concrete strategies that can be customized to address students, teachers, administrators, corporations, non-profit organizations, and human resource departments, along with specific communities of discourse and practices in variable educational situations.

Our notion of democracy, by its very nature and history, suggests that our borders are always expanding and are ever inclusive.[67] And so it must be with leadership education—ever expanding, becoming more and more inclusive and respectful of the other. Emerging leaders at the intersection will need to respond to the question of the other with recognition, respect, and reverence. What a revelation it is to discover not only the values that we hold in common, but to discover that values that are very different from our own can have their own integrity—and that different values and the conflict they engender can provide new and refreshing ways of seeing ourselves and others as part of a larger experiment in living together. If we are—in Kennedy's words— "to retain, reinvigorate and strengthen the American spirit," there must be an "ethic for strangers"[68] that extends beyond conventional understandings of hospitality. Leadership education is the appropriate domain for teaching a new generation of leaders an "ethic for strangers."

BIBLIOGRAPHY

Anderson, J. A. *Driving Change through Diversity and Globalization: Transformative Leadership in the Academy.* Sterling, VA: Stylus, 2008.
Appiah, K. A. *Cosmopolitanism: Ethics in a World of Strangers.* New York: Norton, 2006.
Assmann, J. *Moses the Egyptian: The Memory of Egypt in Western Monotheism.* Cambridge: Harvard University Press, 1999.

67. Lunsford and Ouzgane, *Crossing Borderlands.*
68. Appiah, *Cosmopolitanism.*

Ayers, W. *Teaching the Personal and the Political: Essays on Hope and Justice*. New York: Teachers College Press, 2004.

Banks, J. A., and C. A. M. Banks, editors. *Multicultural Education: Issues and Perspectives*. 6th ed. Hoboken, NJ: Wiley, 2007.

Blasi, A. "Moral Character: A Psychological Approach." In *Character Psychology and Character Education*, edited by D. K. Lapsley and F. C. Power, 67–100. Notre Dame: University of Notre Dame Press, 2005.

Brannon, D. "Character Education: It's a Joint Responsibility." *Kappa Delta Pi Record* 44 (2008) 62–65.

Capra, F. *The Web of Life: A New Scientific Understanding of Living Systems*. New York: Anchor, 1996.

Carter, S. L. *Civility: Manners, Morals, and the Etiquette of Democracy*. New York: Basic Books, 1998.

———. *Integrity*. New York: Basic Books, 1996.

Clark, H. *The Ethical Mysticism of Albert Schweitzer*. Boston: Beacon, 1962.

Cochran-Smith, M. *Walking the Road: Race, Diversity, and Social Justice in Teacher Education*. New York: Teachers College Press, 2004.

Colby, A. "Fostering the Moral and Civic Development of College Students." In *Handbook of Moral and Character Education*, edited by L. P. Nucci and D. Navarez, 391–413. New York: Routledge, 2008.

Cornwall, K. "The Problem with Character Education." (2005) Online: http://patriotismforall.tekcities.com/character_ed.html/.

Cunningham, C. A. "A Certain and Reasoned Art: The Rise and Fall of Character Education in America." In *Character Psychology and Character Education*, edited by D. K. Lapsley and F. C. Power, 166–200. Notre Dame: University of Notre Dame Press, 2005.

———. "The Moral Consequences of John Dewey's Metaphysics." PhD diss., University of Chicago, 1994.

Dalai Lama XIV. *Ethics for the New Millennium*. New York: Riverhead, 1999.

Devall, B., and G. Sessions. *Deep Ecology: Living as If Nature Mattered*. Layton, UT: Gibbs Smith, 1985.

Dilworth, M. E., editor. *Diversity in Teacher Education: New Expectations*. Jossey-Bass Education Series. San Francisco: Jossey-Bass, 1992.

Dreher, D. *The Tao of Personal Leadership*. New York: HarperBusiness, 1996.

Etzioni, A. *The New Golden Rule*. New York: Basic Books, 1996.

Fluker, W. E. "At the Intersection Where Worlds Collide: The Quest for Character, Civility, and Community in Infusing Culture and Diversity in Character Education." Unpublished paper, given as part of the United States Department of Education, Office of Safe and Drug-Free Schools, Partnerships in Character Education Program, Symposium on Emerging Issues in Character Education, Washington, DC, August 18, 2008.

———. *Ethical Leadership: The Quest for Character, Civility, and Community*. Minneapolis: Fortress, 2009.

———. "Recognition, Respectability, and Loyalty: The Quest for Civility among Black Churches." In *A New Day Begun: Black Churches, Public Influences, and American Civic Culture*, edited by R. D. Smith, 139–178. The Public Influences of African American Churches 1. Durham: Duke University Press, 2003.

———. *They Looked for a City: A Comparative Analysis of the Ideal of Community in the Thought of Howard Thurman and Martin Luther King, Jr.* Landham, MD: University Press of America, 1989.

Fluker, W. E., editor. *The Stones That the Builders Rejected: The Development of Ethical Leadership from the Black Church Tradition.* Harrisburg, PA: Trinity, 1998.

Fluker, W. E., and C. Tumber, editors. *A Strange Freedom: The Best of Howard Thurman on Religious Experience and Public Life.* Boston: Beacon, 1998.

Fogel, R. W. *The Fourth Great Awakening and the Future of Egalitarianism.* Chicago: University of Chicago Press, 2000.

Friedman, T. L. *The World Is Flat: A Brief History of the Twenty-First Century.* New York: Farrar, Straus and Giroux, 2005.

Gallien, L. B., and L. Jackson. "Character Development from African-American Perspectives: Toward a Counternarrative Approach." *Journal of Education & Christian Belief* 10 (2006) 129–42.

Gardner, H. *Leading Minds: An Anatomy of Leadership.* New York: Basic Books, 1995.

Goldberg, M. *Kingdom Coming: The Rise of Christian Nationalism.* New York: Norton, 2006.

Goldfarb, J. C. *Civility and Subversion: The Intellectual in Democratic Society.* Cambridge: Cambridge University Press, 1998.

Goleman, D., et al. *Primal Leadership: Realizing the Power of Emotional Intelligence.* Boston: Harvard Business School Press, 2002.

Grosby, S., editor. *The Virtue of Civility: Selected Essays on Liberalism, Tradition, and Civil Society.* Indianapolis: The Liberty Fund, 1997.

Guinier, L. *The Tyranny of the Majority: Fundamental Fairness in Representative Democracy.* New York: Free Press, 1994.

Habermas, J. *The Theory of Communicative Action.* Vol. 2, *Lifeworld and System: A Critique of Functionalist Reason.* Translated by T. McCarthy. Boston: Beacon, 1981.

Hauerwas, S. *A Community of Character: Toward a Constructive Christian Social Ethic.* Notre Dame: University of Notre Dame Press, 1981.

James, W. *The Principles of Psychology*, Vol. I. New York: Dover, 1950.

———. *Talks to Teachers on Psychology and to Students on Some of Life's Ideals.* New York: Holt, 1921.

Josephson Institute, Center for Youth Ethics. CHARACTER COUNTS!® 2008. Online: http://charactercounts.org/.

Kennedy, J. F. *A Nation of Immigrants.* New York: Harper & Row, 1964.

King, M. L. Jr. *Where Do We Go From Here: Chaos or Community?* Boston: Beacon, 1967.

King, P., and H. Devere. *The Challenge to Friendship in Modernity.* London: Cass, 2000.

Lakoff, G. *Don't Think of an Elephant!: Know Your Values and Frame the Debate.* White River Junction, VT: Chelsea Green, 2004.

Lapsley, D. K., and F. C. Power, editors. *Character Psychology and Character Education.* Notre Dame: University of Notre Dame Press, 2005.

Lawrence-Lightfoot, S. *Respect: An Exploration.* Cambridge: Perseus, 2000.

Lehr, D., et al. "Character Education and Students with Disabilities." *Journal of Education* 187 (2006) 71–83.

Lerner, M. *The Politics of Meaning: Restoring Hope and Possibility in an Age of Cynicism.* Reading, MA: Addison-Wesley, 1996.

Levinas, E. *Difficult Freedom: Essays on Judaism.* Translated by S. Hand. Johns Hopkins Jewish Studies. Baltimore: Johns Hopkins University Press, 1990.

Levi-Strauss, C. *Structural Anthropology*. Translated by C. Jacobson and B. G. Schoepf. New York: Basic Books, 1963.

Lickona, T. *Character Matters: How to Help Our Children Develop Good Judgment, Integrity, and Essential Virtues*. New York: Touchstone, 2004.

———. *Educating for Character: How Our Schools Can Teach Respect and Responsibility*. New York: Bantam, 1992.

Lickona, T., et al. "CEP's Eleven Principles of Effective Character Education." (2007) Online: http://www.character.org/uploads/Eleven%20Principles.pdf/.

Lunsford, A. A., and L. Ouzgane, editors. *Crossing Borderlands: Composition and Postcolonial Studies*. Pittsburgh Series in Composition, Literacy, and Culture. Pittsburgh: University of Pittsburgh Press, 2004.

MacIntyre, A. *After Virtue: A Study in Moral Theory*. 2nd ed. Notre Dame: University of Notre Dame Press, 1984.

McCollough, T. E. *The Moral Imagination and Public Life: Raising the Ethical Question in Public Life*. Chatham House Series in Political Thinking. Chatham, NJ: Chatham House, 1991.

Morris, M., and J. A. Weaver, editors. *Difficult Memories: Talk in a (Post) Holocaust Era*. Counterpoints 165. New York: Lang, 2002.

Musil, C. M. "The Shell Game: Regeneration at the Crossroads." An address at the Association of American Colleges and Universities' Diversity and Learning Conference, Philadelphia. October 2006. Available by subscription online: http://www.aacu.org/Podcast/DL06_podcasts.cfm. A summary of the address is online at: http://www.diversityweb.org/Digest/.

Nhat Hanh, T. *Living Buddha, Living Christ*. New York: Riverhead, 1995.

Nash, R. J. *Liberating Scholarly Writing: The Power of Personal Narrative*. New York: Teachers College Press, 2004.

———. "A Post-Modern Reflection on Character Education." In *Character Psychology and Character Education*, edited by D. K. Lapsley and F. C. Power, 245–67. Notre Dame: University of Notre Dame Press, 2005.

Nucci, L., and D. Narvaez, editors. *Handbook of Moral and Character Education*. Educational Psychology Handbook Series. New York: Routledge, 2008.

Pawelski, J. "Pragmatism, Habit Formation, and the Development of Character." Unpublished paper, University of Pennsylvania, 2005.

Putnam, R. D. *Bowling Alone: The Collapse and Revival of American Community*. New York: Simon & Schuster, 2000.

Ricoeur, P. *The Symbolism of Evil*. New York: Harper & Row, 1967.

Roberts, S. "In a Generation, Minorities May be the U.S. Majority," *New York Times*, August 14, 2008.

Rosaen, C. L. "Preparing Teachers for Diverse Classrooms: Creating Public and Private Spaces to Explore Culture Through Poetry Writing." *Teachers College Record* 105 (2003) 1437–85.

Scapp, R. *Teaching Values: Critical Perspectives on Education, Politics, and Culture*. New York: Routledge, 2003.

Schweitzer, A. "The Ethics of Reverence for Life." Originally published in *Christendom* 1 (1936) 225–39. Online: http://www1.chapman.edu/schweitzer/sch.reading4.html/.

———. *The Philosophy of Civilization*. Translated by C. T. Campion. Amherst, NY: Prometheus, 1987.

Senge, P. "Systems." In *Imagine What America Could Be in the 21st Century: Visions of a Better Future From Leading American Thinkers*, edited by M. Williamson, 167–78. Emmaus, PA: Rodale, 2000.

Shields, D. L., and B. L. Bredemeier. "Can Sports Build Character?" In *Character Psychology and Character Education*, edited by D. K. Lapsley and F. C. Power, 121–39. Notre Dame: University of Notre Dame Press, 2005.

Shils, E. "Tradition and Liberty: Antinomy and Interdependence." In *The Virtue of Civility: Selected Essays on Liberalism, Tradition, and Civil Society*, edited by S. Grosby, 103–22. Indianapolis: The Liberty Fund, 1997.

Shusterman, R. "Somaesthetics: A Disciplinary Proposal." *Journal of Aesthetics and Art Criticism* 57 (1999) 299–313. Online: http://www.artsandletters.fau.edu/humanitieschair/somaesthetics.html/.

Smagorinsky, P., and J. Taxel. *The Discourse of Character Education: Culture Wars in the Classroom*. London: Routledge, 2005.

Spalding, E., et al. "The March of Remembrance and Hope: Teaching and Learning about Diversity and Social Justice through the Holocaust." *Teachers College Records* 109 (2007) 1423–1456. Abstract online: http://www.tcrecord.org/content.asp?contentid=13136/.

Takaki, R. T. *From Different Shores: Perspectives on Race and Ethnicity in America*. 2nd ed. New York: Oxford University Press, 1994.

———. *Iron Cages: Race and Culture in 19th-Century America*. New York: Oxford University Press, 2000.

Thomas, L. *Living Morally: A Psychology of Moral Character*. Philadelphia: Temple University Press, 1989.

Thurman, H. *Deep Is the Hunger: Meditations for Apostles of Sensitiveness*. Richmond, IN: Friends United Press, 1978.

———. *The Search for Common Ground*. Richmond, IN: Friends United Press, 2000.

Tisdell, E. J. "In the New Millennium: The Role of Spirituality and the Cultural Imagination in Dealing with Diversity and Equity in the Higher Education Classroom." *Teachers College Records* 109 (2007) 531–60.

Turner, P. A. *Ceramic Uncles & Celluloid Mammies: Black Images and Their Influence on Culture*. New York: Anchor, 1994.

Welch, S. D. *Sweet Dreams in America: Making Ethics and Spirituality Work*. New York: Routledge, 1999.

West, C. *Prophesy Deliverance: An Afro-American Revolutionary Christianity*. Philadelphia: Westminster, 1982.

Williamson, M., editor. *Imagine What America Could Be in the 21st Century: Visions of a Better Future From Leading American Thinkers*. Emmaus, PA: Rodale, 2000.

Wilson, J. Q. *The Moral Sense*. New York: Free Press, 1993.

Wren, T. "Philosophical Moorings." In *Handbook for Moral and Character Education*, edited by L. Nucci and D. Narvaez, 11–29. New York: Routledge, 2008.

Wren, T., and C. Mendoza. "Cultural Identity and Personal Identity: Philosophical Reflections on the Identity Discourse of Social Psychology." In *Moral Development, Self, and Identity*, edited by D. K. Lapsley and D. Narvaez, 239–66. Mahwah, NJ: Erlbaum, 2004.

Zakaria, F. *The Post-American World*. New York: Norton, 2008.

– 2 –

The Ethical Dilemma in Affirmative Action Status

DERRICK BELL

As SOMETHING OF AN honorary alumnus of this school, with my 1995 Candle of Social Justice Award as evidence, I'm really very pleased for this opportunity to return and tell the students and faculty what you already know: that you are most fortunate to be full citizens of the Morehouse College community. Here, in a nation still beset by issues of race, you are the majority; you are at home. "Home is where the heart is," or as one writer put it, "Home is the place that when you go there, they have to let you in."

You can happily come home again as an alumnus of Morehouse College. I remember listening with envy as friends who graduated from black colleges returned year after year to attend homecomings, alumni reunions, and commencements. They discussed their college experiences endlessly and enthusiastically. I have no doubt you will too, when you achieve alumnus status. Enjoy this experience.

I want to talk about the ethical dilemma of affirmative action. I certainly have been both the beneficiary and the victim of affirmative action during my career. And regardless of your superior abilities, most of you also will be both beneficiaries and victims. You will soon face the predicament that I, and so many others, must face and endure.

I went to a mainly white college, and then attended law school in my hometown of Pittsburgh, Pennsylvania. The schools treated me well, and I recognize them publicly for their role in my success. For their part, they willingly extolled my achievements with all manner of honors. But I just don't feel anything like the attachment to my schools that you feel, and will come to feel, for Morehouse. Oh, I give to their fund drives, though likely not as generously or as willingly as you will give to Morehouse once you've followed your predecessors into careers of success and achievement. In the schools I attended I was enrolled, but not really welcomed. You see, I attended college and law school before the era of affirmative action.

You know the history. The Supreme Court's 1954 decision in *Brown v. Board of Education* found racial segregation legally unconstitutional, but the ruling did very little to alter racially discriminatory beliefs and policies. In 1968, in the wake of the murder of Dr. Martin Luther King, Jr., civil rights protests led to the creation of laws requiring desegregation of public facilities.

Most corporations, agencies, and universities remained primarily white and male, but some institutions saw the value in bringing on a select number of white women, blacks, and other people of color. I can tell you, after those initial recruits, the opportunities became quite limited for other minorities wishing to follow suit.

Today, the *Brown* decision is still on the books, but as far as law is concerned, *Brown* is irrelevant. Federal power has been subordinated to state power, just as it was before *Plessy v. Ferguson*. Race has been erased as a legal consideration; its use, whether for benign or remedial purposes, is treated with the same suspicion as an overt racial barrier.

In 2003, the Supreme Court rendered an historic and closely divided verdict on affirmative action in *Grutter v. Bollinger*. The slender 5–4 vote on the University of Michigan Law School's controversial case upheld the school's policy of using race as a factor in admission decisions. The importance of diversity in the student body is cited as a "compelling interest" that justifies the consideration of race.

Under this decision, institutions can independently determine how much diversity is sufficient to meet their needs. This is hardly a victory. My friends Richard Delgado and Jean Stephancic, who coauthored *Critical Race Theory: An Introduction,* said, "As formalism is to conservatives, the diversity rationale in constitutional law is to liberals—a mechanism that papers over a great deal of blood, pain, and death embodied in a 400-year history of racist oppression in favor of a cheerful, forward-looking approach to racial remedies."[1]

Universities, abetted by liberal lawyers and administrators, unerringly select the diversity rationale when conservatives challenge race-conscious admissions and hiring policies. It is easy to see why. The remedial rationale, that the policy is intended to remedy decades of overt discrimination, would require a school to disclose much about its recent past that it would just as soon leave buried. The lives of great figures, whose names grace campus buildings and statues, may reveal a dark side. They might have been slaveholders, or merchants who profited from the slave trade, or leaders of raids against Indians, or . . . you get the point.

Diversity, on the other hand, emerges as a much safer rationale. One can simply make the case that society would be better off with a few more black or Latino engineers—which of course it would—and let it go at that. Not only is diversity a rather pallid, morally unimaginative approach to integration, but it suppresses stories of racism and discrimination in higher education that should be aired and examined. The diversity rationale favored by liberals kills off these stories, making them irrelevant; the province of a few hotheads who want to stir up trouble and are unwilling to let bygones be bygones.

How this works in practice, and the ethical issues raised for its beneficiaries, is illustrated in a book I wrote in 1987, *And We Are Not Saved: The Elusive Quest for Racial Justice*. In the chapter titled, "The Unspoken Limit on Affirmative Action: The Chronicle of the DeVine Gift,"[2] the heroine of many of my stories, Geneva Crenshaw, is ready to resign from her job teaching law. She is exhausted by all the demands made on her time in her unofficial role as advisor, counselor, and advocate on racial issues. She is frustrated by her inability to convince the school to hire more faculty of color. Geneva is visited by a well-dressed black man, Mr. Taylor DeVine, who is the head of a black hair-product company. Mr. DeVine tells Geneva that he understands her problem, and he thinks that he can use his widespread contacts across the country to help her find high-quality minority candidates for faculty positions. He sends Geneva six minority aspirants with outstanding credentials, and the school hires them all.

Then Mr. DeVine, in what he calls "the divine gift," sends a seventh candidate. Though the young black man is an experienced lawyer with

1. Delgado and Stephancic, *Critical Race Theory*, 99.
2. Bell, *And We Are Not Saved*, 140–61.

exceptional qualifications, the law school dean tells Geneva that they will not offer this candidate a job. He suggests instead that the young man apply to their sister school across town.

Geneva is shocked. "I'm not bringing these people here to help the school across town," she says. "I need them here."

The dean calmly tells Geneva, "This is one of the oldest and finest law schools in the country. It simply would not be the same school for our students and the alumni with a predominantly minority faculty—as I thought you, an advocate of affirmative action, would understand."

Geneva is hot. "I am no mathematician, [she] said, but 25 percent is far from a majority. Still, it is more racial integration than you want, even though none of the minorities, excluding perhaps myself, has needed any affirmative-action help to qualify for the job. I also understand, tardily I admit, that you folks never expected that I would find more than a few minorities who could meet your academic qualifications. You never expected that you would have to reveal what has always been your chief qualification—a white face, preferably from an upper-class background."

Geneva threatens to sue, maintaining that her seventh candidate is more qualified than anyone currently on the faculty, regardless of their race. But the dean remains calm. He tells Geneva, " I have discussed this at length with some faculty members, and we realize that you may wish to test this matter in the courts. However, there are precedents for this type of suit."

"I don't wish to be unkind," the dean continues. "We do appreciate your recruitment efforts, but a law school of our caliber and tradition simply cannot afford to look like a professional basketball team."

In protest, Geneva resigns from the school.

When Geneva reports her conversation with the dean to the seventh candidate, he is strangely silent. Then he writes a letter that spells out the dilemma that many of you will face as I have in the workplaces of this country:

> Dear Professor Crenshaw,
>
> Until now, when black people employed race to explain failure, I wondered how they might have fared if they made less noise and done more work. I believed one had to show more harm and shed fewer tears. Embracing self-confidence and eschewing self-pity seems the right formula for success. A commitment to personal resources rather than reliance on public charity seems to me the American way to reach a goal, for blacks as well as whites. I

thought racial bias was not a barrier, but instead a stimulant toward showing others what blacks can do in the workplace.

Now, based on what you've told me, no rationale will salvage what was my philosophy for achievement and my justification for work. My profession is not a bulwark against this destruction. It is instead a stage prop, illuminated with colored lights to mask the ongoing drama of human desolation; a desolation we all suffer regardless of skill, experience or personal creed.

You suggested I challenge my rejection in the courts. But even if I won the case and gained the position to which my abilities entitle me, I would not want to join a group whose oft-stated moral commitment to the meritocracy has been revealed as no more than a hypocritical conceit; a means of elevating those like themselves to elite positions. Their qualifications will never be tested because they do not matter.

The law school faculty may not realize that the cost of rejecting me is exposure to themselves. They are, as Professor Roberto Unger said in another context, "like a priesthood who lost their faith but kept their jobs."

The growing number of highly qualified Asian students is also changing the definition of merit. They pose a similar threat to the elite colleges' status as mainly white institutions. Sadly, my law firm and virtually every other major institution in this country would take the same action as your school in a similar crisis of identity.

But if I condemn hypocrisy in the law school, I must not condone it for myself.

I have thus concluded that I can no longer play a role in this tragic farce. The talent and worth of the few of us who happened to get there first is dangled like bait before the masses. Qualified minorities are led to believe that what can never be done is a real possibility. This system must be forced to recognize what it is doing to you and me—and itself. When next you hear from me, it will be in a new role: as an avenger rather than an apologist.

Yours, the Seventh Candidate.

The letter, while a shock to Geneva, hardly prepared her for the disturbing note that arrived a few days later from DeVine Taylor.

He writes:

Dear Geneva,

Before you received my divine gift, your very presence at the law school posed a major barrier in your efforts to hire additional minority faculty. Having already appointed you, the school relaxed. Its duty was done. Its liberal image was assured. When you suggested the names of other minorities with skills and backgrounds like your own, your success was ignored and those you recommended were rejected.

When my divine gift forced your school to reveal the hidden, but no less substantive, basis for dragging their feet on hiring minorities, the truth became clear. As the token minority law teacher, your employment provided the institution with a façade of respectability far more valuable to them than any aid you provided either to minority students or the cause of black people. You explain your resignation as a protest, but you must realize that removing yourself from that prestigious place was your necessary penance for the inadvertent harm you have inflicted on the race you are sincerely committed to saving.

I'm pleased that my recruitment efforts served the intended purpose. This is my divine gift to you. I wish you every success in your future work.

DeVine Taylor

What does the ethical law teacher do with the lessons contained in this story? I consider my own life's narrative. Like Geneva, I worked hard as a law professor to get more well-qualified minority teachers hired in my schools. I left two tenured positions to protest the schools' failure to employ those I recommended.

I'm hailed for my forthrightness on behalf of people of color. But I wonder if part of my motivation was a quiet, perhaps unconscious realization that my presence was providing those institutions with a racial legitimacy they did not deserve.

Today, as I continue to teach, I am fully aware of the role I play involuntarily. In my story, Geneva Crenshaw resigns and the seventh candidate refuses to pursue a teaching position he no longer wants. What would you do?

W. E. B. DuBois, the legendary civil rights leader, once said, "I have not always been right, but I have always been sincere." We must have the candor and willingness to speak the truth, in both calm and troubled times. None of us can always be right, but we can always seek the sincerity that is based on truth.

Though DuBois spoke the truth about the dilemma of race in America, his words were mostly ignored. As early as 1935, DuBois said we should not push for desegregated schools. What black kids needed, he argued, was neither separate nor integrated schools; what they needed was education. When the Supreme Court ended segregation laws with the *Brown v. Board of Education* case, DuBois predicted that the new law would not be implemented before the educations of millions of black and white children were ruined. Of course, that is exactly what happened.

In 1954, the country was violently divided. On one side were people seeking equality, and on the other side were people happy with the status quo. Blacks, lacking any political or economic power, feared their demand for equality would never be satisfied.

To understand what the Supreme Court did in the case of *Brown*, I refer you to Georgetown Law professor Michael Seidman. He reminds us that the Supreme Court, in taking on the school segregation cases, faced a massive contradiction between the nation's oft-cited commitment to equality and freedom for all, and the great value most white people placed on the racial preferences approved by *Plessy v. Ferguson* in 1896. Seidman explains: "The contradictions and ideology of the 'separate but equal' doctrine were permanently destabilizing and threatened any equilibrium."

The Supreme Court's decision in *Brown* purported to end this destabilizing potential. Seidman says they resolved the contradictions by definitional fiat. Before *Brown*, separate facilities were deemed inherently equal. After *Brown*, separate facilities were proclaimed inherently unequal. The problem with this aphorism was that once white society, by decree of its highest court, made facilities "legally nonseparate," they felt the demand for equality was satisfied. They felt black people no longer had just cause for complaint. The mere existence of *Brown* served to legitimize the current conditions. Thus *Brown*, the definitive legal statement on racial rights, became irrelevant.

Neither Professor Seidman nor I are saying that nothing changed. I could spend hours detailing the things that are better now than in 1954. But there is no escape from the dilemma of life in a racist society. If you look at the statistics today comparing black and white America, black people still fall substantially below the racial curve in employment, income, wealth, education, housing and overall well-being. Even when their status is relatively equal, a sizeable number of white people continue to feel superior to blacks.

Many Americans believe that racism is a thing of the past. They believe that people like me are bellyachers who are making excuses for those who haven't succeeded. I hear it all the time, and you're going to hear it all the time: "You keep talking about all this racism. But you must have faced racism as a black man and look where you are. Why can't the rest of your people be successful like you?"

You will realize: it's not a question, it's a statement of belief. These people believe that the Supreme Court settled all of this 50 years ago. Why else would the 50th anniversary of the *Brown* decision prompt so many programs of commemoration and celebration? Those who speak in these programs add as an afterthought to their remarks, "Of course, there is more work to do . . ." They use statements like this to paper over the fact that schools are now as separate and unequal as they were before 1954. Because of certain court decisions over the last dozen years that are hostile to civil rights, black people have little more protection against today's forms of discrimination than our forebears did in the era before separate but equal, before the standard of *Plessy v. Ferguson* was decided in 1896.

The belief in white superiority remains as viable today as it was in early American history, though it is more subtle in its contemporary form. Take any discrimination case before some of our honored judges who worked in the civil rights field and say, "Your Honor, my precedent for relief is *Brown v. Board of Education*." They may smile weakly, perhaps some will have a tear in their eye, but they won't be able to give you relief because there will be no smoking gun of discrimination. They will say your case is about qualifications and experience, that we already have our share, and so on. It's going to be very difficult to win your case; impossible if all you have going for you is *Brown v. Board of Education*.

Political campaigns feed off the notion of white supremacy. Twenty years ago, Republicans seized control over Southern voters by making vague promises of social reform while emphasizing their determination to protect whites against liberal—read: black—threads, such as school integration and affirmative action. They characterized the Democratic Party as the party for "special interests," a euphemism meaning, of course, the party for blacks. This platform, along with an attack on big government, propelled Ronald Reagan to the White House in 1980. (Reagan's campaign, incidentally, started in Neshoba County, Mississippi. Even those who are not so smart would get that message.)

Sadly, the Democratic leadership, who were absolutely dependent on black votes (particularly in national elections), went to great lengths to avoid acknowledging that reliance. Like Republicans, Democrats sought the elusive white vote by claiming that they were not catering to special interests.

Ironically, if either party were to bring together black and white voters by emphasizing both races' similar needs, interests, and disadvantages, the resulting coalition would be formidable indeed. But the two principal parties show little serious interest in uniting the races, knowing that the obstacles involved would be difficult to overcome in a political campaign.

If you read the platform positions and speeches of both parties in the 2004 electoral campaign, you might conclude that race is not a major issue. I would disagree. Let me illustrate that dispute with a question. Can you think of any black person with President Bush's record who could be reelected instead of facing impeachment? I don't think so. You may have a contrary opinion.

For argument's sake, bring to mind Secretary of State Colin Powell. He is regarded as one of the most respected men in America. Despite his race, both parties considered him for their presidential candidate. He rejected the overtures, but had he accepted . . .

Let's consider a scenario where Powell is chosen for the vice presidential post. Imagine the president is incapacitated or dies, and Powell is sworn in. During his term, he carries out a series of foreign and domestic policies like those of President Bush. After four years, could he seriously run for reelection as opposed to running from impeachment? Think about it.

In different ways, both major political parties are hobbled by racism. Beneath the Republican party's ideological appeal to whites is an identification with President Bush's folksy whiteness. There are a great many whites, and—God help us—some blacks and Hispanics, who ignore President Bush's shortcomings, and even feel comforted by them. They are ready to believe whatever he says, not in defense of his shortcomings, but in defense of him.

The Democrats are reluctant to fight toe-to-toe with President Bush; alas, with good reason. They fear they might trample on some of his protected whiteness, and as a result, lose white votes. The Democrats need the majority of black votes to have any chance of winning the White House, but they refuse to address the continuing issues of race for fear it will cost them white votes.

Still some ask: Is racism alive and well in America? Absolutely. Certainly there is some insulation if you work at a black school or a black-owned business, but you cannot hide from the broader societal condition. Racism is permanent. It is a stabilizing component in a society with great and growing gaps in wealth and opportunity. Rather than give in to despair, let this knowledge make you aware. It will give you an advantage over many whites, and unfortunately, more than a few blacks and other minorities.

The world is a mess, but it's always been that way. I love the Bible story of Peter, who noticed things were going badly all around him. Peter appeals to the Lord, concerned that mankind is not listening to his word. Instead they are worshiping false idols, spending money foolishly, and living worthless lives. Jesus quiets Peter, putting a hand on his shoulder, and says, "Save thyself, the rest are mine."

Wherever you turn after graduation, you will be hard pressed to do right within institutions thriving on wrong. It's tough going out there. You will try to do the honorable thing in an environment where even your righteousness is turned to the advantage of people that you despise. When I became the dean of the University of Oregon law school in 1981, Peter Gomes, who was a Harvard professor and one of the great ministers of our time, spoke at a dinner in my honor hosted by the black students. He said, "Derrick, I want you to keep in mind that as a dean you will be seen as an evil. You will disappoint expectations. You will reward expectations that you should disappoint with your authority, and most of the time you won't know the difference. There is nothing you can do about it except look in the mirror every morning when you wake up and say, 'I am a dean and therefore I am an evil, but today I'm going to try to be a necessary evil.'"

Peter Gomes didn't know very much about how little authority law school deans actually have, but his words apply to all of us. We are the ones who will be out there, working hard and moving on up. People will say, "Well, this one's making it, you're making it . . . how come the rest of them can't make it?" It will not be a question. There is nothing you can do about it except try to be a necessary evil each day on behalf of our people.

In Toni Morrison's novel *Beloved*,[3] the character Denver receives similar advice from her long-departed grandmother. Denver is terrified of white people, and with good reason. In slavery they'd whipped her mother while she was pregnant, crippled her grandmother, jailed her mother, owned everything.

> And all of these memories scared Denver to death. And Denver hadn't left the house for years, but now needing to get help for her sick mother, she stands on the porch trying to get up courage to leave. And she has this imaginary conversation with her grandma, an escaped slave who had told her about how evil whites can be.

3. Morrison, *Beloved*.

"But you said there was no defense!" Denver says, meaning against white people, Semple explained.

"There ain't," says her grandma in her mind.

"Then what do I do?" "Know it, and go on out the yard. Go on."

Not only is this a good philosophy, it may be the only philosophy that makes sense for black people in this country. This philosophy provides a resolution to the dilemma faced by those of us who are considered the beneficiaries of affirmative action policies. We are exploited involuntarily as we benefit. Our interests are served only fortuitously when those interests are in line with the policymakers, who can undo them at a moment's notice. We must know it, then go on.

This experience-based philosophy inspired my book *Faces at the Bottom of the Well: The Permanence of Racism*.[4] The book is used in any number of college courses, and I am afraid it is as relevant today as it was when it was published in 1992. In the epilogue, I wrote that our forebears, betrayed into bondage, survived the slavery that reduced them to property; entitled neither to rights nor to respect as human beings. As the legacy of our spirituals makes clear, our enslaved ancestors somehow managed to retain their humanity, as well as their faith that evil and suffering would not be the extent of their destiny or the destiny of their descendants. They chose to begin and maintain families, even though they knew at any moment the family could be sold and separated, never to see one another again.

Even "free" blacks living in the pre-Civil War North suffered the ever-present knowledge that the Underground Railroad ran both ways. While abolitionists operated the illegal network that helped blacks escape slavery, slave catchers commanded an equally extensive system for kidnapping Northern blacks and spiriting them off to the South for a life in bondage. We owe our existence to the perseverance and faith of our ancestors.

We're proud of our heroes, but we must not forget those whose lives were not marked by extraordinary acts of defiance. Though they lived and died as captives within a system of slave labor, they produced worlds of music, poetry, and art. They reshaped the Christian cosmology to fit their spirits and needs, transforming Protestantism along the way. They produced a single people out of what had been many. Their dignity throughout their ordeal speaks to the indomitable human spirit. That is the real black history, all too easily lost in today's affirmative action debates.

---

4. Bell, *Faces*.

In these times, we are closer than we may realize to those who struggled as slaves. The dangers we black people face in our inner cities are insidious. Persecuted by a callous society (and all too often by others of our race), many young blacks vent their rage on victims like themselves. The crisis perpetuates the terror that whites invented long ago. We should not be surprised that a society that once legalized slavery and pursued fugitive as well as free slaves, now views black-on-black crime as a problem only for its victims and the black communities.

Perhaps those of us who can admit we are imprisoned by the history of racial subordination in America can accept that we have no choice but to accept our fate. It is not that we legitimate the racism of the oppressor; on the contrary, we can only delegitimate it if we can accurately pinpoint it. Racism lies at the center of our society, not at the periphery; in the permanent, not the fleeting; in the real lives of black and white people, not in the sentimental caverns of the mind.

Armed with this knowledge, we can accept the confrontations with evils that we cannot end. We can recognize and acknowledge, at least to ourselves, that any actions we take to abolish racism are unlikely to lead to transcendent change. I believe this is a more realistic perspective from which to gauge the present and future worth of our race-related activities. We can go forth to serve knowing that our action will not change conditions, and may even worsen them. We can have an awareness that our best intentions to help the victims of the system may instead benefit the very system we despise. As Ray Charles reminded us in one of his songs: "Understanding is the best thing in the world, yes it is, yes it is."

Develop for yourselves a philosophy that matches the unique dangers we face, and enables you to recognize opportunities in those dangers for committed living and humane service to others. Find ways to remind the "powers that be" that we are out there. Remind them that we are not on their side, and that we are determined to stand in their way.

This task is less daunting than it might appear. You will learn, just as our people have learned throughout history, to live and work for racial justice in the face of external threats. There are no easy answers in life; only challenges for each generation. By rising to these challenges—winning some, losing others—we gain salvation; not in some other life, but in the here and now.

BIBLIOGRAPHY

Bell, D. *And We Are Not Saved: The Elusive Quest for Racial Justice.* New York: Basic Books, 1989.
———. *Faces at the Bottom of the Well: The Permanence of Racism.* New York: Basic Books, 1993.
Delgado, R., and J. Stefancic. *Critical Race Theory: An Introduction.* Critical America. New York: New York University Press, 2001.
Morrison, T. *Beloved.* New York: Knopf, 1987.

– 3 –

Ethical Leadership for the Twenty-First Century: Science, Technology, and Public Policy

SHIRLEY ANN JACKSON

I THINK THIS MUST be one of the more inspiring assignments I have received—to select a topic that speaks to "issues of integrity, empathy, and hope as moral indices for ethical leadership." Being an academic, I do follow instructions. The issues I will address encompass some that I have encountered in my own experiences in science, technology, and public policy. They involve ethical questions that present when knife-edge issues arise in society. The thread that ties together all of these elements is *leadership*.

Taken on their own, science and technology are essentially neutral commodities. They choose no sides, they offer no judgments, they render no opinions except with respect to the science itself. But science is no stranger to controversy. There are always debates as to the truth and replicability of scientific results and discoveries. The results of research remain neutral until they are applied, when they are ascribed meaning or significance. The truly controversial issues lie at the juncture of science and society, where new knowledge is applied in ways that may have unanticipated moral or ethical implications, where safety or security risks must be balanced against the benefits achieved, where we find public understanding or not, where we may find fears about the use of science and technology. These make up some of the knife-edge issues inherent in the advancement of scientific discovery and technological innovation.

I grew up in Washington, DC in what people today call the "inner city." I am a public high school graduate. My mother taught me and my siblings to read before we began kindergarten. My father drove a taxicab and worked in a post office to support his family. He said, "Reach for the stars so that you can reach the treetops. At any rate, you will get off the ground." My father's message was that if I didn't aim high, I wouldn't go far. I am a scientist today in part because of my parents' partnership.

But I am also a scientist because of two significant events in US history. One was the 1954 *Brown v. Board of Education* decision, which desegregated the public schools. That decision put me (and others like me) into a wider arena, exposing me to greater competition, but also opening my eyes and showing me windows of opportunity that previously would not have been available to me.

The second was the Soviet launch of the Sputnik satellite in 1957. It led the United States into a space race, which, in reality, was a defense-based science race. A lot of attention was placed on identifying young people who had interest and talent in science and math, and putting them on a track to become scientists or engineers.

The convergence of these two events changed my life. I entered the Massachusetts Institute of Technology (MIT) at a time when among the four thousand undergraduates, around ten were African American. There were times where I was shot at and spit on. Everyone shunned me. But I remembered what my father said, and I persevered.

And so it was that I was propelled into a life of science, into a world where the difference between success and failure often means the difference between life and death, especially in the realms of biotechnology and medical science.

About 90 percent of the world's diseases affect the populations of developing nations, but only about 3 percent of research and development worldwide is directed toward those diseases. The bulk of drug development investment is made in treatments for diseases that affect people in developed countries, where costs can be more readily recovered. The system by which we operate—the world in which we live—supports this distribution of resources.

Now consider HIV/AIDS. One of the greatest challenges in treating HIV infection is that the HIV virus continually replicates and mutates, leading to drug resistance. Fuzeon, a groundbreaking HIV/AIDS drug that received US Food and Drug Administration (FDA) approval in March of 2003, shows promise in helping patients overcome this resistance to many of the more commonly used antiretroviral drugs. Fuzeon works because it interferes with the action of a protein called GP41 on the surface of HIV. This protein is what allows the virus to gain entry into CD4 cells. The drug inhibits the ability of the virus to fuse with immune system host cells, thus inhibiting viral replication and helping to restore the patient's natural defenses.

Fuzeon, which was developed by the biotechnology company Trimeris in partnership with Roche Pharmaceuticals, was the first HIV/AIDS drug approved in seven years. (I am proud to say that the team of developers at Trimeris included several alumni of the university that I lead, Rensselaer Polytechnic Institute.) Unfortunately, Fuzeon costs between thirty thousand and forty thousand dollars per patient, per year, putting it out of reach of those without comprehensive health insurance.

You may be wondering why Fuzeon is so expensive. The high costs of funding, and of exploiting, pharmaceutical research and development are key here. The average cost to develop a new drug in the year 2000 was approximately $800 million. We should ask whether patent protection, which is at the heart of our system for developing new pharmaceuticals, yields the best methods for funding research and development, and whether it is the method most likely to produce the best drugs. Looking at the issue from another angle, should the federal government regulate the cost of pharmaceuticals? And if government regulations were enacted, what would such regulations look like?

At the root of these inquiries is the essential question of who benefits from a particular drug. Does the answer to that question affect people's willingness to ensure that the drug reaches those who need it? What are the drug developers' responsibilities to see that patients in need of a drug receive it?

Consider a disease such as leishmaniasis, a parasitic infection transmitted through the bite of an infected sand fly. A deadly version of this infection, visceral leishmaniasis (also known as VL or kala azar), afflicts 1.5 million people around the world, killing two hundred thousand of them every year, primarily in India, Bangladesh, Sudan, Brazil, and Nepal. An antibiotic called *amphotericin B* effectively treats leishmaniasis, but a course of the drug costs $120. This may not sound like much to us, but if you are living in any of the countries I mentioned, $120 is a lot of money.

One solution to the global issue of financial responsibility for drug development was devised by Dr. Victoria Hale, a scientist in the pharmaceutical and biotechnology industries who also served as an FDA official. Dr. Hale knew from her work that many promising drug projects, especially those focused on treating diseases of the poor, do not result in the development of a drug (and the clinical trials that would follow) because of the lack of funding. So she organized the Institute for OneWorld Health (iOWH), the first not-for-profit pharmaceutical company in the United States. The company identifies these so-called orphan drugs—the drugs that have never been completely developed—and negotiates for intellectual property rights, raises development funding, and persuades researchers into contributing their expertise.

Recently, iOWH completed the largest-ever Phase III clinical trial of paromomycin, an off-patent, broad-spectrum aminoglycoside antibiotic with antiparasitic activity. Paromomycin was already known to be effective in treating leishmaniasis, but it had never gone through clinical trials for approval. Clinical trials by iOWH showed that a course of paromomycin is as effective as the other antibiotic, amphotericin B, but only costs about $10 instead of $120. Now iOWH is seeking regulatory approval in India for injectable paromomycin, a once-a-day, 21-day cure for visceral leishmaniasis, which provides lifetime immunity. When approved, paromomycin will be the most affordable therapy for treating visceral leishmaniasis in the world.

What is the point here? Simple. Sometimes it takes thinking outside the box to solve an ethical issue.

Researchers in developing countries conducting clinical trials for new drugs to treat HIV/AIDS, tuberculosis, and malaria, diseases that disproportionally affect developing countries, are coming under criticism for not providing participants with treatment when the trial concludes. The World Medical Association has what is called the Declaration of Helsinki, which lays out guidelines for global medical ethics. It states that patients in a study should be assured of access to the best-proven prophylactic, diagnostic, and therapeutic treatments. The FDA and National Institutes of Health do not adhere to the Declaration of Helsinki principles. Instead, the FDA has proposed alternative guidelines, which critics say are not transparent and do not address issues regarding researchers' potential or actual conflicts of interest. Critics point out that the FDA-proposed guidelines do not require the publication of study results or the post-trial treatment of clinical trial subjects. The ethical question raised by these issues may be framed as follows: Should US government agencies adopt global standards, or are global standards so expensive and restrictive that they would inhibit drug research and development in this country?

Another example of an ethical challenge comes from the area of high biodiversity. Organisms that cannot flee their predators (for example, plants or coral) are evolutionarily predisposed to develop high toxicity. Biologists are now learning that this material, called cyanobacteria, may be developed into drugs for the treatment of human disease. Testing the harvested substance, however, requires equipment that relies on radioactivity, which is difficult to import to developing countries. Dr. Eduardo Ortega, a parasitologist at Panama's Institute for Advanced Scientific Investigations, developed a new testing method. After its DNA is tagged with a fluorescent stain, the parasite is incubated with the cyanobacteria that comes from these toxic substances. If the cyanobacteria under study have no effect, the fluorescence increases as the parasite reproduces. If the fluorescence does not increase, researchers know that they have found bacteria with potential for development as a pharmaceutical. This method is now being used to search for organisms that are active against malaria, Dengue fever, and leishmaniasis.

Interesting questions emerge about who should profit from patents based on biodiversity found in developing countries. If the extracted material were a mineral like diamond, or a heavy metal like gold, there would be little question that the country of origin would receive compensation. Currently, US patent law protects the individuals who do the intellectual work necessary to turn raw biological discoveries into marketable products. International law does not yet address such issues. Should such individuals be able to benefit from their intellectual labor? What is the right ethical position?

My final biomedical example concerns the issue of balancing potentially life-saving but experimental treatment with regulatory oversight. I was once a regulator, but not in this realm. In 2003 a teenage boy was brought into the emergency room at Beaumont Hospital in Royal Oak, Michigan, having been accidentally punctured in the heart with a nail gun. Although physicians repaired the puncture, the boy suffered a massive heart attack and damage to his heart muscle. Physicians transplanted stem cells from his bone marrow into his heart in the hope that the muscle tissue would regenerate. With this procedure, he improved. When the treatment was revealed, however, the FDA forbade further transplantation, pending additional nonhuman studies.

The ability to perform this procedure in the first place resulted from breakthroughs in basic bioscience and tissue engineering. However, the procedure had not gone through the requisite trials and FDA approvals and was therefore extremely risky. What would you have done?

Moving from the medical arena to the nuclear arena, let me tell you about an issue I encountered as chairman of the US Nuclear Regulatory Commission (NRC). The NRC is the successor agency to what was once known as the Atomic Energy Commission. It licenses and regulates all commercial nuclear power reactors, research reactors, test and training reactors, and reactor byproduct materials in the US. It is responsible for the oversight of the transportation, storage, and disposal of radioactive waste, and it is the licensing and export control agency of the United States government. But it is primarily known for its oversight of nuclear power plants.

At the Millstone Nuclear Power Plant in Waterford, Connecticut, questions arose over serious safety issues, specifically during shutdowns, when the full reactor nuclear core was offloaded during refueling. An NRC investigation found numerous instances of nonadherence to safety requirements, some of them quite serious. We gave the utility operating the plant thirty days to show corrections to the safety problems and design-basis issues, and to implement a corrective action program and an employee concerns program. If they failed, then the plants would be shut down, an unusual step for the NRC to take.

In March of 1996, just eight months into my tenure as NRC chairman, a *Time* magazine cover story titled "Blowing the Whistle on Nuclear Safety" took this issue public. It raised concerns over serious safety issues and regulatory practices at Millstone, and by extension, around the country.

As you might imagine, the event caused a crisis of confidence for the NRC. I decided that this was an important learning moment for the agency. The day the *Time* magazine article broke, I addressed all agency employees, and the next day I held a press conference. I did this because the media, public, Congress, and every other constituency needed to know that although I had not been at the NRC when these problems started, I accepted responsibility for the agency. I wanted people to know that although I was not there during the years that these issues were building, I would account for the agency's past, current, and future performance. I wanted to send the message that operational safety in nuclear activities remained the NRC's paramount mission and focus.

Ultimately, I ordered the shutdown of the Millstone Nuclear Power Station, sending reverberations throughout the nuclear power industry. The plant remained closed for two and a half years. One of its reactors was never restarted for economic reasons. A nuclear power plant operated by the same utility, Connecticut Yankee, also was shut down during this period for similar reasons, and it also never reopened.

One does not lightly close down a nuclear power plant. It is a hugely complex undertaking with vast repercussions. It involves millions of dollars in costs to the industry owners. A typical nuclear power plant's revenues for a year are about a billion dollars; costs, when replacement power has to be purchased, are eventually passed along to customers. Closing a plant affects electricity supply to critical care facilities, such as hospitals. It affects the reliability of the energy supply in this country because nuclear plants help to stabilize our electricity grid. A plant closure affects the ability to provide cooling in the heat of the summer. It affects the salaries of hundreds of workers, thus affecting their families' welfare. It affects public confidence in nuclear power generation, the reputations of congressional representatives from the area where the plant is located; and more broadly, a plant closure affects the confidence that Congress and the public have in regulatory oversight and in the safety of nuclear facilities.

During the time that the Millstone Nuclear Power Station was closed, there was enormous pressure from the public to keep the plant shut down, perhaps permanently. On the other hand, there was pressure from plant employees to reopen the facility as quickly as possible because they were worried about losing their jobs. There was pressure from the media, who questioned the performance and credibility of the NRC; and pressure from Congress, whose members were split between those who thought the NRC was being too tough on the nuclear industry and those who thought the agency was not being tough enough.

There was pressure specifically from the Connecticut congressional delegation, whose members had to balance their views on safety with the state's need for nuclear-produced electrical power during two very hot summers. (It seems that Connecticut was not connected well to the rest of the national grid, so it was not easy to import electrical power.) Finally, there was pressure from the NRC staff itself. Some of that pressure was from employees who felt unfairly maligned by the media, and some of the pressure was exerted by employees who did not agree with my tough stance towards the utility or with their fellow NRC staffers. Ultimately, we all came together on what needed to be done.

I testified at a number of congressional hearings and met with Congressional members on all sides of the issue. I had never been in a situation like this. When we shut the plant down and I addressed the public, special security was assigned to me from the federal government, the Sheriff's Department, and the local police because of threats against me.

Along the way, there was reassignment of some NRC staff and the resignation of other staff members, a reorganization of the NRC itself, and significant changes in the agency's approach to nuclear reactor regulation, all of which I initiated and carried out. These changes occurred as the agency was developing a new strategic plan; improving its planning, budgeting, and performance management systems; developing documents for risk-informed, performance-based regulation; and creating a review process for nuclear reactor license renewal. At the same time, I was working to build the International Nuclear Regulators Association (INRA), which brought together regulators from eight countries: Canada, France, Germany, Japan, Spain, Sweden, the UK, and the US.

It was a hugely complex situation at a time of great change and great stress at the agency. Each constituency ultimately had its concerns addressed, and we were able to move on in a positive framework. But this multifaceted sequence of events encompassed multiple lessons.

A derivative issue related to the safety of US nuclear power plants is the secure disposal of spent reactor fuel and high-level radioactive waste. Currently, spent nuclear fuel is stored at seventy or eighty sites around the country, in "spent fuel pools" and in dry casks above ground. Finding a safe repository for spent fuel and waste is a sensitive and complex challenge. The US Geological Survey (USGS) has been using computer modeling of water infiltration and climate conditions to determine whether Nevada's Yucca Mountain, located one hundred miles northwest of Las Vegas, could safety isolate radioactive waste and prevent groundwater contamination.

Recently improprieties in the quality-assurance process being used by geological survey scientists came to light. E-mails between USGS scientists seem to indicate that data was compromised. Ultimately, it will be the responsibility of the NRC to adjudicate the issue. Congressional hearings have already been held and federal agencies are investigating. Whether or not this issue will impact the viability of the Yucca Mountain project is yet to be determined. But the incident highlights how critical it is to have objective and credible science. We must ask: Is the data flawed? Are external pressures influencing what should be objective science? What are the pressures on projects and scientists, from whom do they come, and what are the motivations of those exerting the pressure? How can the scientific process best be protected? How do we come to a reasonable resolution?

What would you do in these instances? How would you resolve these issues if you were in a position of leadership? What resources would you draw upon for guidance? How do integrity, empathy, and hope apply in resolving the complex issues that surface in our increasingly complex world?

Most of these questions encompass change: change from the norm; change stemming from discovery; change in technology, capacity, and orientation. Change is usually difficult. But I have extracted certain principles that help to guide me when I am in a leadership position. I believe these principles could be useful to you.

The first is integrity, which is the state of sound moral principles. More specifically, integrity means upholding the highest standards and setting an ethical example on a continuous basis, despite pressures you face. Everyone must, with integrity, examine his or her own conscience to determine what he or she believes is appropriate action in a specific situation.

I like the definition provided by former Congressman J. C. Watts, Jr. He said, "Integrity is doing the right thing when nobody's looking." There are too many people who think that the only thing that is right is to get by, and the only thing that is wrong is to get caught. A lot of what we see in public life is about wrong being defined as being caught, as opposed to right being what you do when nobody's looking.

The second principle is vision. There are two kinds of vision. There is vision that sets a tone and a direction, and that must be rooted in clear-eyed thinking and in a clear-eyed view of the big picture. Then there is vision to delineate the complex, intertwined ethical questions within their larger context, and their implications for society at large.

The third principle is courage. To lead requires the courage to make—and to stand by—difficult choices, to be willing to face the knife-edge issues, which discovery and innovation often pose in the scientific context. Once a decision is made, courage is needed to stay the course.

The fourth principle is the engagement of others in coming to a principled stand on a difficult issue, and getting others to join you in staying the course. It means engaging constituencies and enlisting participation to enable decision making to profit from multiple insights and creative energies.

The fifth principle is language. The language we choose when we speak about issues is very important. Language sets the tone and can include or exclude. Language has the capacity to elevate the discussion, drawing the best from everybody.

The sixth and final principle involves action. One must be willing to act, not merely to believe. A lot of us talk a good game about what we believe, but to truly believe, you have got to walk the talk. Action is needed to fashion practical approaches, to address knife-edge issues such as those I discussed involving drugs and their availability to treat those with life-threatening illness.

Leadership must adapt to a changing environment. We have technologies today that create instantaneous connectedness between people, requiring new skills and qualities from our leaders. In the past, leadership relied on the strength and determination of a single individual. This still holds, but leadership now also must address greater complexities at multiple levels. Leaders used to be answerable to a relatively small, contained, homogeneous community, which in some ways made ethical leadership easier because you could operate more under the covers. But in today's wireless, hyperlinked, 24/7 online world, leadership challenges are no longer simple because they reach beyond a single community to touch people across the entire planet. (This is what Thomas Friedman refers to as "the flattening" of the world. It's interesting: Columbus went out to see if the world was round. We found out that it is, but now communications have made the world flat.)

Ethical leadership in this environment is ultimately answerable to a global community. For leadership to be effective, it has to take into account a vast array of needs, capacities, skills, backgrounds, perspectives, cultures, languages, and hopes. Yes, hopes, for it is hope that ultimately lifts the human spirit and motivates people to take ethical stands and to act.

How then do we contend with the ethical challenges in this millennium? First of all, be curious. Ask questions and be as informed as you can be, but allow differing ideas and perspectives to stretch your thinking. Creativity, innovation, discovery, and ethical decision making derive from the sensitivities developed from such juxtapositions. Gather around you people from diverse backgrounds, perspectives, experiences, and viewpoints, and when you do that, seek commonalities and new approaches. Let the differences freshen and inform your thinking. Let the differences help you all come together.

Going forward in your lives, you are going to encounter decisions and questions and choices everyday, most of them small and seemingly unimportant. Yet each of them will require a special clarity to see beyond the immediate issue, to contemplate the broader view, to weigh the benefits, to be aware of consequences of decisions, to be informed and knowledgeable, but also strong, inclusive, and able to act with integrity.

And you must be strong. Nothing is ever gained if we are unwilling to take a stand, to be unafraid, to lead by example, to engage others. I have tried to share some specific examples that relate primarily to public policy because I am one who has to live at the intersection of science, technology, and society. I cannot opt out. I could not opt out when I was doing research, I could not opt out when I was chairman of the Nuclear Regulatory Commission, I cannot opt out today as president of Rensselaer Polytechnic Institute or as a member of the board of the New York Stock Exchange.

The bottom line is that what you think must be reflected in what you do, because thinking and action both matter. They reinforce each other. In the end, I believe that each has within us the power and obligation to confront ethical issues, whether one is a designated leader of others or one is leading others by example. Let me close by quoting the great leader, Reverend Dr. Martin Luther King Jr. He was a leader of moral integrity and courage, with the vision to see the ethical path, who called for action with language that engaged a community, and ultimately, a nation. He once said, "Cowardice asks the question, 'Is it safe?' Expediency asks the question, 'Is it politic?' Vanity asks the question, 'Is it popular?' But conscience asks the question, 'Is it right?' And there comes a time when one must take a position that is neither safe, nor politic, nor popular, but [one] must do it because conscience tells [one] it is right."[1]

---

1. Martin Luther King Jr. "The Other America." Speech delivered at Grosse Pointe High School, Grosse Pointe, Michigan, March 14, 1968. Online: http://www.gphistorical.org/mlk/mlkspeech/index.htm/.

– 4 –

Ethics and Leadership: The Challenge of Globalization

JAMES A. JOSEPH

WE STAND TODAY AT an extraordinary moment in American history. On September 10, 2001, there was a real fear that America was becoming isolationist. Our television screens were filled with pictures of demonstrators, mostly from abroad, protesting against globalization. Quietly and with less fanfare, a new anti-internationalism was gaining strength in the United States. Cloaked in claims of sovereignty, the new movement advocated nonparticipation or selective participation in international conferences and protocols. There was a rising tide of unilateralism, even among those who were internationalists. There was a belief that the United States was capable of going it alone, and should be prepared to do so even if it meant disengaging from those international institutions we helped establish.

Everything changed on September 11, 2001, the day the World Trade Center was attacked. The new sovereigntists lost their appeal, and America sought a reengagement with the rest of the world. Multilateralism was back in fashion. Once again, we were willing to say that we had no permanent friends or permanent enemies, only permanent interests. A real effort was made to erase memories of our recent rejection of the almost universally accepted protocol on global warming. As a US ambassador in 1999, I remember the sting of trying to explain our refusal to sign on to the Land Mines Convention, the Senate's rejection of the Comprehensive Test Ban Treaty, and our rejection of the Rome Treaty for the establishment of an international court. I also remember trying to explain why the United States alone stood with Somalia in not acceding to the United Nations Convention on the Rights of the Child (UNCRC). Today may be a new day, but those memories continue to linger in the minds of people in many parts of the world.

It is against this historical backdrop that we examine the topic, "Ethics and Leadership: The Challenge of Globalization." We have already seen in vivid display the importance of context and culture. Leadership scholars are again wrestling with the eternal question, do leaders emerge because of certain traits and skills, or are they shaped by the situation? It is not my purpose to argue for either school of thought, but I want to look at the implications of globalization on how we think about ethics and leadership.

The Fear of Globalization

Let me begin by looking at the fear of globalization. We need to understand that many who reject globalization do so because they see it as essentially "Americanization." Protestors from Seattle to Beijing have denounced what they see as the disastrous effects of globalization (uncontrolled competition) on the fragile economies of Africa, Asia, and Latin America. At the 2001 United Nations Conference on Racism in Durban, South Africa, which focused on xenophobia and racial discrimination, globalization was characterized as promoting and perpetuating the prejudices and intolerance of Western society.

Should we fear globalization? No. Should we be concerned about it? Yes, argues UN Secretary-General Kofi Annan. "The poor are poor not because of too much globalization, but because of too little," Annan said. "Not because they are part of it, but because they are excluded."

From an American perspective, it is easy to observe the benefits of the global flow of capital, technology, and people. It is easy for us to see the advantages of eliminating barriers to trade and travel. But the voices proclaiming the dangers of globalization are getting louder and more concerning.

The increasing international discontent falls into two basic categories. The first involves the economic and political downsides of globalization for developing economies. The financial volatility and corrupt leadership in some underdeveloped countries have caused a severe recession and an increase in inequality within and among nations.

The second category of discontent over globalization involves a crisis of expectation. Many new leaders of emerging democracies began their preparation to take power when it was believed that nation states, including developing nations, could manage their economies in ways that would encourage a free market. As they assumed power, however, they found the ground had shifted and their economies were greatly affected by outside forces they could not control.

In the end, no nation can avoid the challenge of globalization. As we embrace the advantages globalization offers, the United States will need to help ease the anxieties it generates.

The Globalization of Civil Society

The first stage of globalization was primarily political. The cold war divisions brought rival nations together across national political boundaries in a brand new way, creating allies of former adversaries and adversaries of former allies.

The second stage of globalization was economic. Nations with very different political interests found themselves tied together by an interdependent world economy. Trade, investment, and the transfer of technology opened formerly closed borders, and more and more nations chose to participate in global integration for the sake of mutually assured prosperity.

The third stage saw the globalization of civil society. Some of the most influential leaders in the international arena emerged at this time from nongovernmental organizations. That is why I find it difficult to understand how so many people misread the impact of the UN Conference on Racism. One American magazine described the conference as "the disgrace in Durban." Another saw it as largely a failure. I wish the conference had been able to deal with a more comprehensive set of issues—for example, the problems of Afro-Latinos in Latin America, the Kurds in Turkey, the untouchables in India, the indigenous people in Australia—but I would not agree that the conference was a total failure.

I prefer to see those who are frustrated and justifiably angered by their predicament engaged in rhetoric rather than violence. We may not have liked some of the things we heard in Durban, but it provided a forum rather than a battlefield. All of us should have learned something from the passion let loose before and after the conference. We should now have a feel for the frustration of the large numbers of people who are desperately seeking some sign that the rest of the world cares. The legacy of the intentional underdevelopment of a people is all around us. We ignore it at our peril.

For me, the story of the UN Conference is the vacuum created by the United States' failure to lead. I wish the US had chosen to remain engaged. I believe that the highly respected US Secretary of State, Colin Powell, could have taken it further. This was an opportunity to talk sensibly about reconciliation and reparation, to shift the conversation away from individual compensation to assisted self-reliance and participatory development. In our absence, the South Africans and others willing to search for common ground took the conference light-years ahead from where it began.

Was the conference a failure? I think not. We have the beginning of a global anti-racism movement where it belongs—with the institutions of civil society. Let us not forget the role that civil society played in the collapse of Communism, the fall of the Berlin Wall, and the ending of apartheid. Governments will only address the issues of racial discrimination and related intolerance if the people demand it. Durban may have been the beginning of a global demand.

The Emergence of Soft Power

We come now to the impact of globalization on leadership: the emergence of soft power. In a July 1999 article in *Foreign Affairs*, Professor Joseph Nye, who heads the Harvard Kennedy School of Government, explained the important distinction between "hard power" and "soft power." Hard power refers to the use of military might or economic muscle to influence, even coerce. Soft power refers to the ability to attract and influence through the flow of information and the appeal of social, cultural, and moral messages. Hard power is the ability to get others *to do what we want*. Soft power is the ability to get others *to want what we do*.[1] The former is based on coercion, while the latter is based on attraction.

Military power in the world is unipolar, with the United States outstripping all other countries. Economic power is multipolar, with the United States, Japan, and Europe accounting for two-thirds of the world's production. Soft power is more widely dispersed. The flow of information crosses borders and does not depend on military or economic power. That

---

1. Nye, "Redefining the National Interest."

is why social and moral values may be the most fundamental and significant source of soft power. A compelling message from a disaster area, a gross human rights violation, a military conflict, or a story of hope and healing conveyed by the Internet or television: any of these can easily catapult new priorities into a nation's foreign policy.

In 1981 President Ronald Reagan alluded to America as the "shining city on the hill," a utopian emblem of productivity and peace. The power that comes from being the "shining city on the hill" does not provide the coercive capability with which most Americans identify, but in the new age of national security, soft power can sometimes be the most influential. International systems are changing in many ways, and more discussion is needed to understand the implications for American power and influence.

I saw the impact of soft power firsthand during my tenure as the US Ambassador to South Africa. Nelson Mandela, the first democratically elected president of South Africa, was the epitome of soft power. His influence came from the strength of his humanity and the elegance of his spirit. It came from his message of reconciliation and the moral instinct embodied in his spirit of forgiveness. Mandela is the prototype of the leader whose influence comes not from military or economic might but from the power of ideals and from the ability to capture the minds and hearts of people in all corners of the world. Among the many lessons we should learn from the life and legacy of Nelson Mandela is that diplomacy increasingly depends on a moral ecology that cannot be found in military or economic power.

The Shift from a Cold War to a Hot Peace

I particularly like the way Chinese scholar Wang Jisi describes the era of soft power. He writes about the shift from a "cold war" to a "hot peace."[2] "Hot peace" refers to a world in which cooperation and opposition coexist. There would be a collage of fractured interests that don't quite cohere but can endure friction. The collage would hang together in some loose order because the attraction would remain stronger than the repulsion.

Unlike international conflict in the twentieth century, which was modern, ideological, and totalitarian, conflict in the twenty-first century is predicted to be postmodern, partial, and nonideological. By unilaterally asserting its own interests, the United States is causing other nations to see their own interests more clearly. They are banding together against the

2. Wang, "'Hot Peace'—Not Cold War—Between the US and China."

US based on shared interests. Even traditional allies are reassessing their relationships with the United States. It is increasingly clear that the global influence of the US will be significantly eroded if it seeks to unilaterally shape world order rather than collegiately engage other nations.

The tragedy of September 11th reminded us how important it is to be prepared to exercise hard power. But I hope it also reminded us of the necessity for soft power in the world of the twenty-first century. Combating global terrorism is more than an issue of military might. If the enemy is hatred, rather than a people or a place, our leaders will need to look more deeply, and more comprehensively, at the emotions driving the worldview of the United States, especially in those countries that now concern us. Those emotions range from frustration, resentment, and anger, to hatred, hopelessness, and fanaticism.

Greater pluralism in the mobilization and use of soft power may diminish the ability of the United States to impose its will through the use of hard power. However, the appeal of our institutions, the freedom of our society, and the values we espouse should continue to give us an edge in the new world of soft power. While our people and leaders recognize that American military and economic advantages are great, they must also acknowledge that hard power is neither unqualified nor permanent.

If we have learned anything from those who are building new societies in Eastern Europe, South Africa, and Central America, it is that the next generation of leaders is unlikely to fit the traditional mold or to emerge from traditional places. Their styles will be different. Their accents will be different. Their colors and complexions will be different too.

But what about their values? How will they cope with the challenges of globalization? Can they apply ethics to public life without getting caught up in the politics of virtue or the parochialism of dogma? Will these new leaders be able to borrow from the best of the prevailing leadership paradigms while learning to appreciate the differences imposed by culture and context? How can they provide hope and healing to a world integrating and fragmenting at the same time? These are a few of the questions that leadership scholars should be asking as they study leadership in a global context.

Private Virtues and Public Values

I want to shift gears and address a question posed by Socrates: "What is a virtuous man and what is a virtuous society?" Of course, today we are more likely to ask: "What is a virtuous man or woman, and is it possible to build a virtuous society?" It is not my intention to try and answer these questions here, but I do want to put forth this assertion: The focus on private virtues that saw the emergence of a small but noisy group of virtuecrats near the end of the last century is likely to be matched in the new millennium by a focus on the public values that drive institutions and empower leaders.

Why this renewed preoccupation with values in public life? Francis Fukayama, who burst into national attention a few years ago with a book titled *The End of History*, has written a new book, *The Great Disruption: Human Nature and the Reconstitution of Social Order*. Fukayama draws on the latest sociological data and theoretical models from fields as diverse as economics and biology to argue that though the old order has broken apart, a new social order is already taking shape. Western society, he contends, is weaving together a new fabric of social and moral values appropriate to the changed realities of the postindustrial world.

To restate Fukayama's argument in my own language is to say that for more than a decade now, we have been preoccupied with the micro-ethics of individual behavior, the private virtues that build character. We now must give equal attention to the macro-ethics of large institutions and systems, the public values that build community. You may not agree with the tactics of demonstrators who gather at the World Bank and International Monetary Fund meetings, but it should not deflect from the reality that more and more people are concerned about how large institutions impact their cultures, communities, and general well-being. They want to know whether or not these governing institutions have a moral center.

For some time, we have been romanticizing small local units as faster, more focused, more flexible, more friendly, and more fun—to borrow the five *F*s that have made the rounds of organizational theory. According to this view, small units can best get close to the customer, member, or citizen. They can be less bureaucratic and more personal. Local groups tend to share a history and a geographic tie. They can identify with their neighbors, and they know each other's faces.

However, we live today in an age of nongeographic communities and huge systems—organized global communications, organized industrial production, organized bureaucracies, organized benevolence, and even organized crime. We will need to balance our natural preference for the small and informal with an understanding of:

- when it is necessary to have organized systems;
- when it is necessary to have a strong center in order to adequately and effectively service the parts; and
- what social values are appropriate for whatever options we choose.

How should a global discourse on values in public life take place? I am increasingly convinced that the first thing we need to do is depoliticize the public discussion of values, to help make it less partisan. It is all too often the case that those who speak the loudest about promoting "good values" are those who simply want to argue that someone else has "bad values." It is time for us to apply the concept of virtue in ways that uplift rather than downgrade, heal rather than hurt, build rather than destroy.

To allow for a national discourse about values, we need to emphasize a new generation of moral habits. In *The Book of Virtues*, conservative pundit William Bennett identifies ten virtues that he considers essential to good character: self-discipline, compassion, responsibility, friendship, work, courage, perseverance, honesty, loyalty, and faith. While this is a good list, we cannot permit the discussion of values to focus only on the micro-ethics of individual behavior. We need to be equally concerned with the macro-ethics of large social institutions, including government, business, and civil society, which are now playing a major role in shaping public policy and priorities. Much has been made of the breakdown of families, but aside from the writings of the largely academic communitarian thinkers, not enough attention has been given to the breakdown of communities and how social virtues often serve as a prerequisite to the development of individual virtues.

So what would a lexicon of public virtues look like? A few years ago, the Kettering Foundation asked a public opinion polling firm to survey American perceptions of multiculturalism and diversity. The first question asked what it meant to be an American. The respondents did not answer in terms of geography or genetics, ideology or theology; most defined their American identity by their commitment to a set of values.

When the question was first put forward, people responded in terms of freedom—freedom of speech, religion, and the economic marketplace. After deliberating for a while, they expanded their definition of American identity to include an array of other values, such as tolerance, respect for others, and even the appreciation of diversity. The pollsters concluded that bringing a dissimilar group together to consider a common identity makes people more sensitive to diversity. Author Amatai Etzioni, founder of the Communitarian Network, a nonprofit organization dedicated to "shoring up the moral, social and political foundations of society," has thus called for a megalogue—society-wide dialogues that link community dialogues into one national conversation.

Bennett's private virtues constitute a good starting point for identifying rudimentary forms of private morality. While they are indispensable for individuals, far more is needed for a complex community or an interdependent society to thrive. The problems of public life are greatly aggravated when we cannot develop direct personal relationships with the people and systems we need. Personal responsibility is in many ways diluted. The directors of a corporation are individual persons, for example, but they are asked to think as directors or shareholders. The private virtues to which they are committed may help them assess and monitor the private behavior of the chief executive, but where are they to find moral guidance in deciding on dividends, the welfare of workers, or the obligation to the community in which the company operates?

The decision about dividends, like the decision about profits, is likely to be regarded as morally neutral. But is it? If a decision affects the welfare of people, it is likely to require moral judgment, and cannot be neatly separated from moral choices.

Adam Smith, the eighteenth-century author of *The Wealth of Nations*, is best remembered as an economic theorist. But he was a moral philosopher before he was an economist. He wrote *A Theory of Moral Sentiments* before he wrote his better-known work on economics. His economic theories were based on his ideas about moral community, especially the notion that the individual has the moral duty to have regard for his fellow human beings.

When Smith studied the personal manner of business transactions between people, he set forth the principle of empathy—the ability to feel what another person is feeling. Knowing what gives others joy because we know what gives us joy became the unstated basis for his economic treatise in *The Wealth of Nations*.

Fukayama also ties social values to economic prosperity. In his second book, *Trust: The Social Virtues and the Creation of Prosperity*, he argues that there is a relationship between the prosperity of nations and social values such as trust. The greatness of this country, he maintains, was built not on the imagined ethos of individualism, but on the cohesiveness of its civil associations, the strength of its communities, and the moral bonds of social trust. He warns that a radical departure from that tradition holds more peril for the future of American prosperity than any competition from abroad. Both Adam Smith and Francis Fukayama argue that the affirmation and practice of certain public values are not only a moral imperative, but in our national interest.

Like Smith, I would begin my own list of public values with empathy. Empathy is a prerequisite for compassion and is fundamental to building community. In a more innocent age we might have described this notion of trust and regard for the other as the associated virtues of love. But love—once the central imperative of social ethics—seems to have been banished from the public discussion of values. We rarely ask in government, business, or civil society, what is the most loving thing to do?

It may be useful to remember that in Plato's inquiry, he came to associate virtue with goodness. In one of his dialogues, Socrates meets the eminent Sophist Protagoras, who explains that his profession is the teaching of goodness. In the subsequent exchange, the foundation of moral imperatives that was laid has come to undergird the notion of civil society. The emphasis is not simply on *knowing* the good, but on *doing* the good.

It is, thus, not surprising that in Plato's *Republic*, the concern with virtue focuses on justice and kindness. Yet, today's virtuecrats rarely mention justice. Like the *L* word, *love*, the *J* word, *justice*, seems to be missing in action. Love thy neighbor as one loves thyself is still good advice. But an abstract value void of committed action does little to establish justice, ensure domestic tranquility, or promote the general welfare. Without a commitment to the promise of justice and the practice of kindness, virtue remains a concept with little context.

I am delighted that Bennett included compassion on his list because it has become an important part of our national discourse on leadership. The most often repeated example of compassion is the story of the Good Samaritan in the New Testament of the Bible. A traveler comes upon a man on the side of the road who is badly beaten. He stops and provides aid and comfort. But suppose this same man traveled the same road for a week, and each day he discovered someone badly beaten in the same spot. Wouldn't he be compelled to ask who has responsibility for policing the road? His initial act of compassion must inevitably lead to public policy. It is this progression from individual compassion to public action that is often missing in our discussion of private virtue. Genuine compassion requires not only that we ameliorate consequences, but that we also seek to eliminate causes.

Ethics as Power

It is not an overstatement to say that ethics have been used historically to domesticate and humanize power. Now we live in a world where ethics *constitute* power. Long before the founding of the American republic, Montesquieu explained that "virtue" is the distinctive characteristic of a republic, as "honor" is of a monarchy and "moderation" of an aristocracy.[3] I would say much the same thing now about values. We cannot long preserve the public ethos of America's founding without the simple understanding that while we used ethics to *domesticate* and *humanize* power through much of the twentieth century, in the twenty-first century ethics *is* power.

It is not only governments that must understand that values constitute the essence of soft power. The same is true of multinational business. Companies must learn that gaining influence is not simply about what they stand *against*, but frequently about what they stand *for*. In my experiences as an officer of a transnational corporation and an advocate for American business abroad, I found that a sound set of principles can affect the bottom line in at least five ways:

1. Principles build trust between a company and a community. That trust translates into loyalty, consistency, and greater productivity.

2. Principles demonstrate that companies are only as good as their people and policies. A company is what it rewards. It must represent more than a mission statement or a code of conduct by valuing its employees. The performance review and reward system must reflect the values the company espouses.

3. Customers and consumers like to know that they are doing business with not only a company that produces quality goods or services, but one that is committed to fairness, honesty, and integrity in the larger community. As international competition increases, companies that perform ethically may have a competitive edge in certain countries.

4. Shareholders are increasingly concerned about company values. Investors have increasingly shown a desire to align their investments with their personal beliefs.[4] Socially conscious investing represents $1 of every $11 invested in professionally managed assets in the United

---

3. Himmelfarb, *One Nation, Two Cultures*, 19.
4. Benjamin, "Assets Jump 18% in Socially Conscious Investments."

States; in 2006, socially conscious investment assets were valued at $2.7 trillion.[5]

5. Self-regulation can make government regulation unnecessary. When I was the president of the Council on Foundations, I frequently testified before congressional committees on proposed legislation to regulate foundations. I often found a more sympathetic audience when I could show that foundations were not only concerned about the matter under discussion, but were also engaged in self-regulation.

Does responsible behavior influence the bottom line? I am convinced that it does. I believe that in the years ahead, there will be increasing evidence that principles have a powerful, practical, and immediate impact on profits.

Ethics and Leadership

We can learn a lot from the South African people about ethics and leadership. Their emphasis on reconciliation may be at the heart of our search for appropriate public values in a world that is both integrating and fragmenting simultaneously. To live together in community is to be constantly engaged in connecting or reconnecting with those who differ not simply by race or religion, but by tradition, theology, politics, and philosophy.

Where there is diversity, there is likely to be alienation and separation. Conflicts are inevitable. Social relationships are constantly threatened and broken. The estrangement that individuals and communities face can be moral, social, or political. Reconciliation involves reestablishing or sustaining a connection to a wider community. There is an implicit notion of brokenness, a relationship that needs to be built or rebuilt. Reconciliation thus becomes as highly prized a value in the age of interdependence as freedom was in the scramble for independence.

In South Africa, reconciliation is both a public value and a public process. It is infused into the political culture of those who govern, the theology of those who claim a new moral authority, and the ancestral tradition of those who now have the lead in building a new society. The commitment to a reconciling society has deep roots in the African experience. In the worst days of apartheid, the African National Congress wrote into its charter that

5. Ibid.

South Africa belongs to all who live in it. These words also found their way into South Africa's new constitution.

There is among black South Africans a traditional concept of community, called *ubuntu*. It assumes that all humanity is bound together in a relationship bigger than any individual or group. This notion of community is best expressed in an Xhosi proverb that Archbishop Desmond Tutu likes to quote: "People are people through other people." It follows that to deny the dignity, or seek to diminish the humanity, of another person is to destroy one's own humanity.

This message is needed so desperately in a world where the more interdependent we become, the more people turn inward to smaller communities of meaning and memory. They feel the tug of separateness from the larger community, of ultimate loyalties devoted exclusively to their own group. It is only natural to feel an affinity with those with whom they share a special heritage. They are demanding respect for their primary community of history and heritage before they can more fully embrace a larger community of function and formality.

At first glance, there appears to be reason for anxiety and despair. But I am increasingly convinced as I travel around the world that the search for beginnings, the focus on remembering and regrouping, may simply be a necessary and natural stage in the search for common ground. Yet, with so many pressing needs within the American borders and beyond, it is time that we learn to see ourselves not through the haze of parochial emotions, but against the backdrop of a larger vision and as part of a larger community.

So let me conclude by suggesting that we can neither understand nor appreciate the changing role of ethics in the public life of the global community without first trying to understand the many voices urging a return of respect for the spiritual dimension. We must try to understand why religion is playing such a large role in public life. Many people, whether they are Buddhist, Muslim, Christian, Jewish, or some other expression of spiritual connection, are coming to believe that we are not here alone, that we do not exist for ourselves alone, that we are a part of something bigger and more mysterious than ourselves.

It is not yet clear what role religion will play in the search for either common ground or public values, but there are many reasons to believe that the search for a higher level of being is a reflection of the human condition. It may be that it is the common search, rather than our different answers, that will provide the basis of our unity.

As we look to the future, it is clear that the ethical issues with which our leaders now struggle are tame compared to some of the issues on the horizon. It is now reliably predicted, for example, that within five years either a US government agency or a private corporation (perhaps both) will have in a desktop computer the entire human gene decoded. Policy analysts and ethicists will then be arguing over the implications of extending the human lifespan for Americans beyond 150 years, at the same time that the AIDS virus and other infectious diseases devastate populations in Africa and elsewhere. I hope that the emerging community of leadership educators, the institutes they develop, and the students whom they teach, will be prepared to handle the new generation of public policy issues as well as the old.

But even more fundamentally, I hope the leadership industry is prepared to handle the diversity that will characterize our leaders in the new millennium. We do not yet know much about these emerging leaders, but we know enough about the changing role of ethics in public life to suggest at least these four conclusions:

1. Global changes in demographics are intensifying the demand for new leaders who understand sharing power rather than dominating with it.

2. Tomorrow's leaders must be able to use their values not only to affirm absolutes but also to cope with ambiguities. In matters of faith and morals, the right question is usually more important than the right answer to the wrong question.

3. It is imperative that leaders develop the capacity for humility. Our world desperately needs leaders who are able to accept the possibility of error in themselves, and who are willing to receive wisdom from unlikely sources. The challenge of leadership is to identify those who share a commitment to the same goals and to make them allies rather than adversaries.

4. Our leaders must be empathetic. Empathy with others, such as those who are economically disadvantaged or politically disenfranchised, will provide the social cement to bind people together in community.

In the midst of the pessimism about some of today's leaders, I find inspiration. I think of Albert Camus, the Existentialist philosopher who described hope as "the faint flutter of [dove's] wings" sounding above the "uproar of empires and nations." I think of Robert Kennedy's "million points of daring."[6] I think of the "servant leader" described by philosopher Robert Greenleaf—the person who sets out to serve and leadership is what follows.

I hope, therefore, that in all of our study of leadership development, behavior, and relationships, we will not forget that in its essence, ethical leadership is about service. Ethical leadership is, in the words of John Winthrop, about "making the condition of others our own."

BIBLIOGRAPHY

Benjamin, J. "Assets Jump 18% in Socially Conscious Investments." *Investment News*, March 10, 2008. Online: http://www.investmentnews.com/article/20080310/REG/782570549/.
Himmelfarb, G. *One Nation, Two Cultures*. New York: Vintage, 1999.
Kennedy, R. F. "The Day of Affirmation." Speech delivered at the University of Cape Town, South Africa, June 6, 1966.
Nye, J. S. "Redefining the National Interest," *Foreign Affairs* 78/4 (1999) 22–36.
Wang, J. "'Hot Peace'—Not Cold War—Between the US and China." *New Perspectives Quarterly* 18/3 (2001) 16–19.

6. R. F. Kennedy, "The Day of Affirmation."

– 5 –

Challenging the Status Quo for Ethical Leadership

MELVINIA KING and BRYANT MARKS

A REVIEW OF MEDIA headlines from the past two decades reveals the challenges of ethical leadership during this period. In the top news stories in 1992, the timeline starts with Clinton's election as president, the Los Angeles riots, and the US intervention in Somalia.[1] Five years later in 1997, the top stories were Princess Diana's death, the conviction and sentencing of Oklahoma City bomber Timothy McVeigh, and the death of Mother Teresa.[2] As we shift to 2002, the stories were President Bush casting Iraq as part of an "axis of evil" and the DC sniper attacks at suburban gas stations and strip malls.[3] Continuing with this trend, the headlines for 2007 ranged from the massacre at Virginia Tech to the state of emergency in Pakistan to the mortgage crisis.[4] From 2008 to 2011, ethical concerns were catapulted to even greater heights with headlines on the economic bailouts, presidential elections, rising unemployment, environmental issues, health care reform, Occupy Wall Street, foreign policies, and revamping the educational system.

1. "Clinton Victory, LA Riots."
2. Boorstein, "Diana, Mother Teresa and McVeigh."
3. "Year in Review 2002."
4. "Year in Review 2007."

Many of the problems identified by these headlines, often caused by and mired in systemic conditions, are reflections of much deeper social ills. These challenges range from personal accountability based on our skewed value systems to our understating the impact of decisions by "ethically challenged" organizational leaders, especially policymakers. *With the public demanding ethical change,* this paper supports the research findings of the Ethical Leadership Model® as a valuable tool for preparing a new generation of leaders. These are individuals who are embodied with a value system, intellectually stimulated, and equipped to flourish while making fitting decisions during these challenging times.

Perhaps the most promising response to public demands for change in leadership comes from those scholars working with approaches in ethical leadership, servant leadership, and transformational leadership. In narrowing this focus, research findings support the Ethical Leadership Model® as significant in developing college curriculums and leadership-training programs.[5] Derived from a study conducted from 1993 to 1997, this approach is based on the role of story; the power of imagination, tradition, and traditionalism. During that time period, models for the transformation of personal consciousness were often lacking the role of ethics in human development. This basic argument for prevention and intervention strategies is that human development requires an ethical anchor, a structure in which leaders themselves must be central participants. The argument expands by emphasizing how self-destructive behaviors and lack of social responsibility to others are symptomatic of a ruptured ethical center. This ethical center shapes and enlightens a leader's sense of self in relation to others and to the universe as a whole. Walter Fluker stresses that any leadership program that seeks to spark a transformation of consciousness must first help leaders engage and repair their ethical centers.[6] This argument is both relevant and timely in supporting current research on ethics. Both Howard Gardner and D. C. Poff emphasize the significance of this leadership approach. Gardner wrote that every profession has an ethical core and that the ethical worker seeks to honor this by always asking: "Am I proceeding in a way that, if others knew just what I was doing, I would be proud or embarrassed?"[7] This can be asked of a broker seeking to provide financial security for a client or a coach seeking to win games for a college. The recent events with Occupy

5. King, *African American Moral Tradition.*
6. Fluker, "Ground Has Shifted."
7. Gardner, "Multiple Lenses."

Wall Street and the Penn State sexual abuse scandal have caused many organizations and leaders to *look hard* at this question. One can presume that individuals involved in these events would be aware of the consequences of their actions. Unfortunately, presumption alone is not enough to deter negative outcomes. Poff takes a more action-based approach (with the philosopher Aristotle) by stating that a virtuous life is part of habituation and education. It must be lived through experience and by acting in virtuous ways. It is both internally driven by the well-educated virtuous person and externally driven by those wishing to be treated fairly and justly.[8] This raises the issue of labeling responsibility. Should universities be responsible for educating future leaders on ethics and moral duty? Challenging the status quo of systems supporting the "educated person" as contrasted with the "educated citizen with a social conscious" is the augmentative strategy delivered by the ethical leadership approach discussed in this paper.

A select group of leaders, characterized as being courageous change agents while using new and innovative approaches within their institutions, were called upon to meet with President Obama.[9] Although these university presidents and thought leaders discussed rising college costs and strategies to improve quality, this meeting also highlighted the importance of organizational leaders not losing sight of personal and social responsibilities. Most often the choice presented to leadership is not between right and wrong, but between what is more right and what is less right. According to Fluker, ethical leaders come into being through the development of character, civility, and a sense of community. He states that this triune of virtues, values, and virtuosities is the bedrock for genuine human development, productivity, and peaceful coexistence.[10] The innovative approach supported by a foundation, corporation, and collegiate precollege ethical leadership program provides a successful strategic model as a tool in leaders choosing between two rights.

Rushworth Kidder describes situations of choosing between two rights as ethical dilemmas.[11] He identifies four models of ethical dilemmas as commonplace. The first model is truth versus loyalty, which exposes one's character when honestly answering questions that could compromise confidentiality or promises to others. The second model is justice versus mercy,

8. Poff, "Ethical Leadership."
9. De Vise, "Obama Meets with Star Presidents."
10. Fluker, "Preparing Students."
11. Kidder, *How Good People Make Tough Choices.*

which exposes acts of civility towards others when deciding to excuse wrong deeds committed under duress or extenuating circumstances. The third model is individual versus community, which exposes creating a sense of community when protecting the confidentiality of information that could be potentially damaging to the greater community. The fourth and last model is short-term versus long-term, which exposes organizations and individuals balancing these models as ethical leaders in spending time implementing current programs as compared with investments in innovative approaches that may provide greater benefits for our global environment in the future. The purpose of this paper is to share an innovative approach by providing the origin and history of the Ethical Leadership Model,® the program structure, and ways in which assessment is being used in supporting the program.

Origin and History of the Ethical Leadership Model®

Within a year of completing a dissertation, Fluker published a book titled *They Looked for a City: A Comparative Analysis of the Ideal of Community in the Thought of Howard Thurman and Martin Luther King, Jr.*[12] The findings from his study not only convinced him that King and Thurman were world-class leaders, but also that they were tied to a particular tradition of discourse and practice.[13] This tradition, called the black church tradition, is also termed the "African American moral tradition" and cuts across politics, sociology, mythology, and aesthetics. The study reveals that in order for leaders to be like Thurman or King, which is to say, ethical leaders, one cannot be cut off from tradition. Hitler was part of a tradition, so it was not quite adequate for Fluker to look only at traditions, but also at the internal habits and practices of those traditions. A fundamental question is: "What were the social practices that conspired to create leaders who had deep concern about justice and social transformation?" Thurman and King were cited as excellent examples. But Fluker later discovered that they were but part of a much larger community of extraordinary vibrant black discourse and practice that reached back for as much as two and a half centuries. The study revealed that Thurman and King were members of an educated, black elite by whose language and discourse the thinking of these individuals was profoundly shaped. Fluker became aware that, while King and Thurman were spiritually moored in the black church tradition, even that tradition

12. Fluker, *They Looked for a City*.
13. King, *African American Moral Tradition*.

intersected with outlier communities of discourse and practice. The most important of these wider communities might be called "modernism" or "liberal democracy," and what some, like Thurman, call "ethical culture."

Insight into genuine human development provides concepts and language used in developing the Ethical Leadership Model®. The type of language that emerged from the study had a great deal to do with shaping Thurman as a leader. Fluker wrote that Thurman was, perhaps, more thoroughly pragmatic and was closer to pragmatism in the sense of John Dewey, and maybe of William James, than he was tied into some of the practices normally associated with the black church tradition. In looking at tradition, social practices, and habits, it slowly occurred to Fluker that in order to have these vibrant habits and practices, and to be able to sustain them over time, one needs strong institutions. The institutions in this case were the black church and historically black colleges and universities. Great leaders such as Thurman, Mordecai Wyatt Johnson, Ella Baker, and others whom we are still modeling had their early formation in these institutions, and especially in historically black colleges and universities. Although there is current growth in research on ethics and leadership,[14] it is interesting to note that Fluker used the term "ethical leadership" before reading one piece of literature. This is noteworthy due to the sparse and disjointed research on ethical leadership during the origination period of his study.[15] This is also noteworthy because he was trying to name the phenomenon discovered in his own research. The collective excitement for his work in ethical leadership led to conversations with the W. C. Kellogg Foundation, which funded this original work.

The concept of African American moral tradition was developed and originally used as an ethical leadership program at Colgate Rochester Crozer Divinity School.[16] In summarizing this section, the original research explores Howard Thurman and Martin Luther King Jr. and their ideas on community. In exploring their lives, focus was placed on practices tied to the black church tradition. While acknowledging the importance of traditions, this work also recognized the limitations and inadequacies of focusing only on traditions. The social practices leading to the formation of great black leaders from earlier historical periods also led to class differentiation leading

---

14. Brown and Trevino, "Ethical Leadership"; De Hoogh and Hartog, "Ethical and Despotic Leadership"; Van Quaquebeke and Eckloff, "Defining Respectful Leadership."

15. Ciualla, *Ethics*.

16. Fluker, "A Proposal to the W. K. Kellogg Foundation."

to opportunities for new language and discourse. By examining Thurman in relationship to Dewey and James, this research showed stronger tendencies for Thurman to be more like these individuals than the traditional practices associated with the black church. This discovery supports an understanding of the formation of habits and practices as being sustained by strong institutions, namely the black church and especially historically black colleges and universities. More so, this research is timely in supporting the innovative action-based approach embracing the philosophy of Aristotle's virtuous life as part of habituation and education.[17] The need for a triune model of virtues, values, and virtuosities based on outstanding habits and practices is supported by research, as well as internationally by corporations, community organizations, and educational institutions for curriculum development and ethical-leadership training programs.

Implementation of the Ethical Leadership Model®: The 2010 Pre-College Leadership Program, Morehouse College

According to A. P. Finley, the powerful lesson for institutions regarding their efforts toward transformational change is not only that these elements are needed, but that assessment is at the heart of each plan. She contends that it is through assessment that we can look critically beyond highly visible institutional problems to what may be more systemic issues.[18] Her narrative-based approach to assessment challenges individuals undertaking institutional change to first seek the voices and then to tell the story of students learning in their organizations. In taking this challenge, this next section will provide an overview of a precollege ethical leadership program and the role that assessment provides in rendering this program transformative.

Program Overview

The 2010 Coca Cola Pre-College Leadership Program (PLP) was conducted at Morehouse College under the direction of Dr. Walter Fluker and Dr. Melvinia King from June 19th through June 26th, 2010. The program was designed to introduce African American male high school students from across the United States to the traits, skills, and behaviors necessary for

---

17. Poff, "Ethical Leadership."
18. Finley, "Assessment and Evaluative Studies."

effective leadership in the twenty-first century. To this end, the program implemented various activities and presented information based upon Fluker's Ethical Leadership Model®. The primary dimensions of the model are *community* (comprising *courage, justice,* and *compassion*), *character* (comprising *integrity, empathy,* and *hope*), and *civility* (comprising *reverence, respect,* and *recognition*). The model asserts that developing and demonstrating the primary dimensions, and related subdimensions, are critical to ethical leadership. The PLP schedule was full and balanced. Activities typically began at or before 9 am and carried into the evening (with the appropriate breaks and downtime). Most of the activities were highly interactive and engaging. The staff included professors, Morehouse College upperclassmen (peer leaders), and individuals with relevant expertise regarding a variety of topics.

Methods

Sample

A total of twenty-nine American males from across the country participated in the program; twenty-eight identified as African American and one identified himself as White American. The participants varied in socio-economic background; 14% were poor to working class, 65% were middle class, and 21% were upper-middle class. The average age of the participants was 16.41 years old. Participant hometowns were distributed as follows: 24% urban, 17% small city, 48% suburban, and 10% rural. All of the participants resided in single-gender residence halls on the Morehouse College campus throughout the program.

Procedure

A mixed methodology design was used to assess the impact of the PLP on leadership development. This approach involved quantitative strategies (i.e., surveys) and qualitative strategies (i.e., focus groups). The fifteen-minute survey comprised items that assessed the primary dimensions (i.e., character, community, and civility) and nine subdimensions (three per primary dimension) of Fluker's Ethical Leadership Model®. The survey was administered during the first day (as a pretest) and last day (as a post-test) of the program. Five focus groups were conducted during the last morning of the program. The sessions were led by a social psychologist with expertise in human development and education and four of his research associates. Participants were asked ten questions (with some follow-up prompts for specificity): a set of three questions for each of the three primary ethical leadership dimensions, and one general question about the impact of the program. The duration of the focus groups ranged from thirty-five minutes to one hour.

Dependent Measures

The survey items and focus group questions that assessed each of the nine subdimensions of the Ethical Leadership Model® were created specifically for this study. The survey comprised original items.

Results

Survey (Quantitative) Analysis

It is important to note that the response scales for all of the survey measures were in Likert form (e.g., strongly disagree ... strongly agree, not at all true ... very true), but varied from four response options to seven response options depending on the particular measure. Thus, all scores were mathematically adjusted to range from 1–5. The adjustment allowed for clear interpretation of results and each of the measures to carry equal weight when collapsed into macrovariables (discussed below). Although the pretest and post-test scores are numerically close to each other, the five-point range of possible scores results in small numerical differences equating to meaningful and often statistically significant differences.

To obtain a more comprehensive understanding of the impact that the PLP had on the survey measures of the three primary dimensions of Ethical Leadership—character, civility, and community—the scores of the subdimensions that make up each of the primary dimensions were averaged together to create a composite measure of the three primary dimensions (macrovariables).

A statistical technique entitled *paired samples t-test* was utilized to assess survey data, which was completely quantitative in nature. When conducting statistical analysis of quantitative data, researchers attempt to determine whether differences between pretests and post-tests are due to chance or to the treatment/experience to which the participant was exposed. Traditionally, researchers consider a difference in pretest/post-test scores (and most other quantitative statistical tests) to be statistically significant if the probability of a difference occurring by chance is 5% or less (i.e., p<.05). Given the small number of participants (twenty-eight participants completed both the pre- and post-tests), a power analysis revealed that the sample was too small to adequately detect statistically significant differences in the scores on the pre- and post-tests. Consequently, scores will be compared descriptively, but we will occasionally mention results that did indeed reach traditional statistical significance.

Focus Group (Qualitative) Analysis

The audio-recorded focus group (qualitative) data was analyzed using *grounded theory*, a technique very commonly used by qualitative researchers. The "p<.05" standard that applies to quantitative data does not typically apply to qualitative data. Instead, the grounded theory approach, which involves grouping responses into themes based upon content and frequency of responses, was used. Because individual response frequencies are calculated during the analysis process, one participant's response can yield multiple frequencies. While this was not typically the case, this possibility must be acknowledged in order to truly understand the nature of qualitative data. It is also important to mention that while all participants were present for the focus groups, not all of them responded to every question. In addition, the results do not tend to reflect responses that: 1) were given by only one person, 2) contradicted other responses, 3) were not audible, 4) did not communicate a clear thought or sentiment, or 5) were in the form of nonverbal communication (e.g., nodding the head) or simple conversational support of a statement (e.g., "mm hmm" or "yes" following another participant's comment). Consequently, the results below represent common themes but are not designed to communicate what every person in each group stated, and thus, frequencies will not typically add up to 29 (i.e., the total number of focus group participants).

DIMENSION 1: CHARACTER

The program had a positive impact on two of the three subdimensions of character—*integrity* and *empathy*. The subdimension *hope* was unchanged. Combining the scores of these subdimensions generated an index variable—an overall score for the character dimension. Scores on the post-test were indeed higher than on the pretest, indicating a positive effect of the program on character.

In order to better understand the effect the program had on the *integrity* subdimension of character, participants were asked, "Did you learn more about yourself during the program? If so, what did you learn?" Twenty-five participants stated that they either learned more about themselves or added more depth to traits and characteristics of which they had previously been aware. Participants responded with statements like: "I thought about stuff that I already knew about myself," "I learned that I wear a mask," and "I learned to look into my heart and see who I was." Only three participants stated that they had not learned anything about themselves. One participant stated, "I think everyone likes me for who I am." The most common theme among the participants was the concept of wearing a "mask." The "mask" that is frequently mentioned refers to portraying oneself as something one isn't. Participants mentioned, "I realized I was wearing a mask with some of my friends and family," and "usually back at home I have to act like somebody else." This lesson caused participants to realize who they were as individual human beings. Fifteen participants shared their personal examples of wearing a mask, while five participants spoke of developing leadership skills, six mentioned positive attitudes, and four described the ability to work with others.

When asked the question regarding the *empathy* subdimension of character, "Were you able to see things from another person's perspective?," thirteen participants stated that they were able to do so. Participants stated, "I felt that I could relate to some of [my brother's] problems" and "empathy is so important to leadership."

Regarding the *hope* subdimension of character, most participants stated they were hopeful about the future in response to the question: "Did the program make you more hopeful about the future?" Twenty-five participants mentioned that they were more hopeful or excited. Of those, eighteen gave candid feedback that centered on being highly ambitious to achieve future goals (ten participants), motivation to attend college (four participants), and being an ethical leader (three participants). One participant stated, "The peer leaders inspired me to be like them or to do better than them." Another said, "Now I know a bit more of what it takes to be a leader." In regards to preparing for his future, one participant shared the following: "It helped me to think out my future goals and plan for them, and right now I still have time to think them over."

DIMENSION 2: CIVILITY

The scores on the measures of the subdimensions of civility—*reverence, respect,* and *recognition*—increased as a result of the program, but only the *respect* subdimension reached traditional statistical significance. Combining the three subdimensions, however, resulted in a statistically significant increase in overall civility from pretest to post-test.

Regarding the *reverence* subdimension of the civility dimension, focus group participants were asked: "Did the program increase your ability to be aware of the people around you and how your comments and behavior might affect them?" In response, twenty participants answered in the affirmative. One participant stated, "being rude just makes you look bad, especially if you want to be a leader."

In order to obtain insight regarding the *respect* subdimension of the civility dimension, participants were asked: "How would you describe the general level of respect among the participants?" Fifteen participants expressed positive feedback. Comments included the following: "even though we had our problems we were able to stop and defuse them." A student mentioned the value of respect that the program taught, saying, "the way that you act or look at them [the staff] can be disrespectful." They were also asked: "Did you feel respected by participants in the program?" The overwhelming majority stated that they did.

In terms of the final subdimension of civility, *recognition*, fourteen participants stated that during the program they had to sometimes put their personal feelings aside for the good of the group or to complete a task. Eleven of those students provided examples. One student explained, "There is a time and season for everything." Another student described the challenge he faced: "I felt uncomfortable when we did [mask making], but I guess I just had to trust my partner." Most of the students who mentioned having to put personal feelings aside indicated that the situation involved their religious beliefs. A student described his concern: "we had done some rituals and I wasn't sure of their origin." A discussion of hip-hop culture was the cause of growth for another student. He shared, "I'm not a big fan of hip-hop but I put those feelings aside and learned a lot from the discussion." Another participant reflected on the development he saw taking place, saying, "they finally progressed and got used to the people and the program."

DIMENSION 3: COMMUNITY

The scores on the measures of the subdimensions of community—*courage, justice,* and *compassion*—as well as the composite variable of overall community increased as a result of the program.

The focus group question related to *courage* was, "Do you think that the program affected your ability to remain true to yourself even when you encountered challenges?" Fourteen of the sixteen participants who responded to this question stated that they remained true to who they were, even if their identity changed during the program (which it did for many). One participant observed, "The program kind of helped me find my true self. Like through face masking. During the revealing of the mask, I didn't really think my personality could have changed. But me taking off my mask helped me to change my behavior."

The focus group question related to *justice* was, "Did the program affect your overall sense of fairness towards others?" Six participants said yes. One participant said, "I had to change the way I view people and be openminded. Don't get me wrong, I learned stuff it just wasn't always fun." Twelve students stated that the program did not affect their sense of fairness. The general reply from these students can be summed up by one participant's response: "I was raised to treat others right." One student mentioned, "I received a compliment from another student for being nice." While students stated the program did not affect their fairness towards others, it was frequently mentioned that the way they perceive others has changed. A student stated, "it changed my perspective on how I view people, and how I deal with them in certain situations. I can take a step back and look at the positive aspect."

Finally, participants were asked, "Did any of you give or receive an act of *compassion* or deep concern by other participants? Please provide an example." The participants shared a general sense of community with the vast majority of them expressing that they gave or received an act of compassion or deep concern. Over half of those participants provided personal accounts of compassion. One student stated, "I really felt compassion for the two brothers that had grandfathers who had Alzheimer's." Another participant stated, "Some people gave away things that were extremely important to them."

Conclusions

The purpose of this study was to determine whether the Pre-College Leadership Program increased ethical leadership as described in Walter Fluker's Ethical Leadership Model®. Both the quantitative (i.e., survey) and qualitative (i.e., focus group) data clearly indicate that the program was indeed effective. Not only were leadership skills enhanced; participants in the focus groups also reported having learned a great deal about the cultures of other people and about various topics in general. It is quite impressive, and rarely the case, that a week-long training program has such a profound effect on participants. The research team witnessed the parting ceremony that included gift exchanges, lots of hugging, and many tears. The researchers concluded that the program was life-impacting and will be fondly remembered by participants for the rest of their lives.

BIBLIOGRAPHY

Boorstein, M. "Diana, Mother Teresa and McVeigh Conviction Top Stories of 1997." Online: http://www.boston.com/globe/packages/year_in_review/news/.

Brown, M. E., and L. K. Trevino. "Ethical Leadership: A Review and Future Directions." *Leadership Quarterly* 4 (2006) 595–616.

Ciualla, J. B. *Ethics, the Heart of Leadership.* 2nd ed. Westport, CT: Praeger, 2004.

"Clinton Victory, LA Riots, Hurricane Lead List of Year's Top News Stories." Online: http://www.deseretnews.com/article/266800/1992--CLINTON-VICTORY-LA-RIOTS-HURRICANE-LEAD-LIST-OF-YEARS--TOP-NEWS-STORIES.html.

Cable News Network. "Year in Review 2002." Online: http://www.cnn.com/SPECIALS/2002/yir/.

———. "Year in Review 2007." Online: http://www.cnn.com/SPECIALS/2007/year.in.review/your.picks/.

De Hoogh, A. H. B., and D. N. Den Hartog. "Ethical and Despotic Leadership, Relationships with Leader's Social Responsibility, Top Management Team Effectiveness and Subordinates' Optimism: A Multi-Method Study." *Leadership Quarterly* (2008) 297–311.

De Vise, D. "Obama Meets with Star Presidents to Talk Reform." Online: http://www.washingtonpost.com/blogs/college-inc/post/obama-meets-with-star-presidents-to-talk-reform/2011/12/05/gIQAFtJoWO_blog.html/.

Finley, A. P. "Assessment and Evaluative Studies as Change Agents in the Academy." In *Transforming Undergraduate Education: Theory That Compels and Practices That Succeed,* edited by Donald W. Harward, 159–71. Lanham, MD: Rowman & Littlefield, 2011.

Fluker, W. E. "The Ground Has Shifted." Unpublished manuscript excerpt taken from *The African American Moral Tradition as a Resource for Leadership Education* by Melvinia T. King. Lewiston, NY: Mellen, 2005.

———. "Preparing Students for Ethical Complexity at the Intersection Where Worlds Collide." *Liberal Education* 97/3–4 (2011). Online: http://www.aacu.org/liberaleducation/le-sufa11/fluker.cfm/.

———. "A Proposal to the W. K. Kellogg Foundation." National Resource Center for Ethical Leadership. Rochester, NY: Colgate Rochester Divinity School, 1991.

———. *They Looked for a City: A Comparative Analysis of the Ideal of Community in the Thought of Howard Thurman and Martin Luther King, Jr.* Lanham, MD: University Press of America, 1989.

Gardner, H. "Multiple Lenses on The Mind." Paper presented at the ExpoGestion Conference, Bogotá, Colombia, May 25, 2005.

Kidder, R. *How Good People Make Tough Choices: Resolving the Dilemmas of Ethical Living.* New York: HarperCollins, 1995.

King, M. T. *The African American Moral Tradition as a Resource for Leadership Education.* Lewiston, NY: Mellen, 2009.

Poff, D. C. "Ethical Leadership and Global Citizenship: Considerations for a Just and Sustainable Future." *Journal of Business Ethics* 93 (2010) 9–14.

Van Quaquebeke, N., and T. Eckloff. "Defining Respectful Leadership: What It Is, How It Can be Measured, and Another Glimpse at What It Is Related To." *Journal of Business Ethics* 91 (2010) 343–58.

– 6 –

The Role of Ethical Behavior in the Elimination of Disparities in Health

DAVID SATCHER, MD

IN JANUARY 2000, WHILE serving as Surgeon General and Assistant Secretary for Health, I released the report *Healthy People 2010—The Nation's Health Plan for the Last Decade*.[1] There were only two goals for Healthy People 2010, consistent with our desire that the American people would be able to remember and embrace the goals.

The first goal targeted healthy aging: the goal was to increase not only the years of life that Americans lived, but also the quality of that life. The second goal was the goal of reducing and ultimately eliminating disparities in health among different racial, ethnic, and socio-economic groups.

Upon release of these goals of *Healthy People 2010*, we acknowledged that these goals could only be achieved with reform in our health system and a new focus on the social environment in which people lived.

During the last decade, there were major developments that impacted these goals both negatively and positively. Perhaps the major negative impact on these goals derived from the economic downturn, which resulted

---

1. US Department of Health and Human Services, *Healthy People 2010*.

in the adding of millions of Americans to the rolls of the uninsured—at least fifty million by 2010.

But there were also some very positive developments. In 2008, Congress passed, and President Bush signed, the Mental Health Parity Act. This was a major recommendation of our *Surgeon General's Report on Mental Health,* which we released in December 1999.[2]

Second, the World Health Organization's (WHO's) Commission on Social Determinants of Health, on which I served, released its report in November 2008 and WHO confirmed it in January 2009.[3] This report documented the critical need to target social determinants of health: the conditions in which people are born, grow, learn, work, and age. Along with this release of the commission's report came the announcement by WHO of its goal of achieving global health equity in the next generation.

Third, Congress passed, and President Obama signed, the Patient Protection and Affordable Care Act (PPACA) in March/April 2009.[4]

The Patient Protection and Affordable Care Act includes a commitment to dramatically reduce the numbers of the uninsured by enrolling at least thirty-two million more Americans in health insurance plans by 2016. The Act also incentivizes primary care and preventive services as well as community-based prevention. Perhaps the most controversial and most challenged component of the PPACA was the mandate that individuals purchase health insurance. Clearly, if upheld and fully implemented, the PPACA will greatly expedite the fulfillment of our commitment to reduce and ultimately eliminate disparities in health, but it alone will not be enough.

Eliminating disparities in health requires us as a nation to rise to a new level of ethical leadership and ethical behavior. In his book, *Ethical Leadership: The Quest for Character, Civility, and Community,*[5] Walter Fluker looks at ethical behavior from three perspectives or dimensions. First, ethical behavior emanates from basic individual integrity. We are challenged to be trustworthy, to be who we say we are, to be consistent, and to make the best of who we are.

Second, ethical behavior is about our interaction with other people; it is a challenge to treat others with civility and respect, as we would like to be

2. US Department of Health and Human Services, *Mental Health: A Report of the Surgeon General.*
3. World Health Organization, *Closing the Gap in a Generation.*
4. US Congress, *Patient Protection and Affordable Care Act.*
5. Fluker, *Ethical Leadership.*

treated. In medicine, this goes beyond the admonition to "do no harm," and requires healthcare professionals to do our best to optimize and maximize the health of our patients and our community.

The third dimension of ethical behavior identified by Fluker deals with our role as members of the community and our responsibility therein. We purchase insurance not just to protect ourselves but to live in an environment where risks are shared and individuals are not overly burdened when faced with acute or chronic illness, including those with which some individuals are born. We support individual mandates as a realization that citizens of a community are joined in protecting each other from such risks.

Our commitment to reduce, and ultimately to eliminate, disparities in health is a commitment to ethical behavior within ourselves, toward each other, and within our community. Disparities in health among different racial, ethnic, socioeconomic, mental health, and sexual health groups are real and they are measurable. They are also reducible, and indeed, preventable.

In the United States, we have reliable data that show a major gap between the chances of an African American baby surviving the first year of life and a majority baby. Infant mortality rates are two and a half times higher for African Americans than for whites.[6] American Indians have the highest risk of diabetes in the US. The risk is lower to African Americans and Hispanics as compared to American Indians, but higher as compared to risks faced by the majority population. However, African Americans have the highest mortality rate from diabetes. This is analogous to the fact that while white women in America have the highest incidence of breast cancer, African American women have the highest mortality rate from breast cancer, due to several issues related to healthcare but also to the nature of the breast cancer involved.

Similar data are available from deaths from cardiovascular disease and cancer, where African Americans have higher mortality rates for all of the four leading cancer causes of death: lung, colon, breast, and prostate.

In a study that we conducted at the Morehouse School of Medicine, the findings of which were published in the *Journal of Health Affairs* in 2005,[7] we looked at mortality rates from all causes, comparing African Americans and whites. Based on these mortality ratios in the year 2000 alone, there were 83,500 excess deaths among African Americans. In other words, if we had successfully eliminated disparities in health in the last century, there

---

6. Satcher et al., "What If We Were Equal?" 460.
7. Ibid.

would have been 83,500 fewer deaths among African Americans in the year 2000 alone. Additionally, between 1990 and 2000, there would have been almost 900,000 fewer excess deaths among African Americans.

Thus, we see that disparities in health are real, and they are measurable within countries but also between countries. Whereas Norway has an infant mortality rate of approximately two per one thousand births, Sierra Leone has a rate of 150 deaths per 1,000 births. The World Health Organization's[8] commitment to health equity in the next generation thus faces a major challenge but not an insurmountable one.

But disparities in health are not beyond remedy. Locally, nationally, and globally, the elimination of disparities in health will require a commitment to the three dimensions of ethical behavior and ethical leadership in our healthcare system and in systems throughout the world.

I am optimistic that the individual-mandate component of the PPACA will be upheld by the Supreme Court. However, regardless of the outcome of the legal challenge to that component of the PPACA, we must move forward with healthcare system reform, and I believe that we will.

Beyond healthcare reform, we are also challenged to reform the social determinants of health, as outlined in the WHO report of 2008 referred to above. Without such reform, we will not eliminate disparities in health or achieve global health equity in the next generation.

In our 2005 study published in the *Journal of Health Affairs*, in addition to noting excess deaths, we showed differences in the mortality ratios between African American men and white men in the United States over the last forty years. Such differences were not apparent in mortality ratios between African American women and white women. African American women showed significant progress in reducing the mortality ratios relative to white women, and life expectancy differences had decreased. The variable most closely associated with the reduction in mortality ratios was the improvement in the educational and related socioeconomic status for African American women. It is clear that intervention that impacts on the social determinants of health must be a major part of the strategy for reducing, and ultimately eliminating, disparities in health. It is gratifying to know that *Healthy People 2020* specifically targets the social determinants of health among its four goals.[9]

---

8. See the World Health Organization website: http://www.who.int/.
9. US Department of Health and Human Services, *Healthy People 2020*.

It is especially critical that we improve the social conditions that impact our children, especially during the periods of pregnancy and prenatally. The environment of the womb is sensitive to nutrition, violence, stress, and toxins, and it must be protected and supported if children are to get a healthy start in life. In fact, as we stated in an article in the *Journal of Health Affairs* in 2010, the baby's brain is virtually sculpted by the baby's nutritional experience in utero.

Likewise, the interaction between newborns and parents must be optimal in terms of support and communication if children are to develop healthy bodies and minds. As a nation, we must invest in programs that result in healthier pregnancies and healthier newborns. This is probably both the most cost-effective, and the most humane and ethical, investment that we can make.

One of the programs of the Satcher Health Leadership Institute engages parents from a very low-income community, 80 percent of them single parents, in a program to improve the quality of parenting. The program is designed with a belief that by enhancing the quality of parenting, we can promote children's mental health, and improve their behavior in early childhood, including school performance. Parent leadership has developed well in this program, and we are optimistic about the outcome.

A study by Felton Earls and his colleagues at the Harvard School of Public Health examines the impact of children witnessing violence at an early age, especially between the ages of three and five. They found that children who witnessed violence (such as murder) at an early age were twice as likely to be victims or perpetrators of the same type of violence before they were adults.[10]

As members of the WHO Commission on Social Determinants of Health, we visited several countries to examine the impact of social determinants of health on health outcomes. One of the most interesting visits was to Chile.

In Chile we were invited to examine a program that specifically targeted poverty and related social determinants of health on health outcomes. From the age of three months, the children of the poor in Chile—especially the lower 10th percentile—were provided access to daycare and later to early childhood education with good nutrition and health interventions. The theory underlying the program is that in the long term, this investment in childhood nutrition, education, and health will save on the costs

---

10. Buka et al., "Youth Exposure to Violence."

of treating diseases. It is also believed that as a result of this program, less money will need to be spent on the criminal justice system. It is still early, but already there are positive signs. It is the type of program that needs to be investigated much more broadly.

We know that poverty, violence, social exclusion (including racism), unemployment, low wages, and lack of access to healthcare and wellness programs all negatively impact health outcomes.

It will take ethical leadership to target these social determinants of health and to work to create the kind of environments where health is ultimately served.

In December 2001, I released the *Surgeon General's Call to Action to Prevent and Reduce Overweight and Obesity*.[11] In that report, we pointed out that as a nation, we had experienced a dramatic increase in overweight and obesity in one generation, 1980–2000. In fact, in children and adolescents, overweight and obesity had doubled during this generation. We admonished the American people to improve nutrition and to become more physically active with their children. We targeted the settings of home, community, school, workplace, and healthcare institutions, and the media, to take actions that would change behaviors that are threatening our future. After leaving government, I worked with a group to develop a program called "Action For Healthy Kids,"[12] the goal of which is to help children develop lifetime habits of physical activity and good nutrition, specifically working with schools, where children spend much of their time. The program was designed with the hope that over time, the group would form a relationship with parents, who would be encouraged to ensure that their children's healthy behavior was carried on at home and in the community.

But as we have struggled to reverse the obesity trend, it has become clear that the social determinants of health are the major barriers we face. If there are no grocery stores with fresh fruits and vegetables in the community, fast food restaurants set the nutrition standards.

If communities are not safe and violence is rampant, it is difficult to motivate outdoor behavior, such as walking, jogging, swimming, or playing ball. In the absence of appropriate resources even in our schools, we cannot require physical education K-12, and it is difficult to model good nutrition. Community ethics demands that we provide safe environments for all of

---

11. US Department of Health and Human Services, *The Surgeon General's Call to Action to Prevent and Decrease Overweight and Obesity*.

12. http://www.actionforhealthykids.org/.

our children and that they are assured access to good nutrition, healthy foods at home and school, and yes—that they are able to develop lifetime habits of physical activity and good nutrition.

The motto of the Satcher Health Leadership Institute at the Morehouse School of Medicine (SHLI/MSM) follows from our mission: "in order to eliminate disparities in health we need leaders who care enough, know enough, will do enough, and who will persist until the job is done."

When it comes to the commitment to eliminate disparities in health, perhaps the most important ethical ingredient of leadership is caring. In fact, healthcare is the only endeavor where caring is incorporated into its name. But it has become increasingly clear, especially from the perspective of social determinants of health, that the need and role of caring is not limited to those in health professions but involves all whose work and other endeavors impact health outcome, directly or indirectly.

The Satcher Health Leadership Institute at the Morehouse School of Medicine is committed to identifying individuals who care enough about health disparities and to provide them with the added knowledge, skills, and motivation to become leaders in this effort. Some of them will be professional leaders, such as physicians, public health leaders, or mental health specialists. Others will be community leaders who live and work in the community. But what they will all have in common is this commitment to the reduction and ultimate elimination of disparities in health based on deep-seated caring.

BIBLIOGRAPHY

Action for Healthy Kids. Online: http://www.actionforhealthykids.org/.
Buka, T. L. et al. "Youth Exposure to Violence: Prevalence, Risks, and Consequences." *American Journal of Orthopsychiatry* 71/3 (2001) 298–310.
Commission on Social Determinants of Health. *Closing the Gap in a Generation: Health Equity Through Action on the Social Determinants of Health. Final Report of the Commission on Social Determinants of Health*. Geneva: World Health Organization, 2008.
Fluker, W. E. *Ethical Leadership: The Quest for Character, Civility, and Community*. Minneapolis: Fortress, 2009.
Satcher, D., et al. "What If We Were Equal? A Comparison of the Black-White Mortality Gap in 1960 and 2000." *Health Affairs* 24/2 (2005) 459–64.
US Congress. HR 3590. *Patient Protection and Affordable Care Act*. 111th Congress. 2009.
US Department of Health and Human Services. *Healthy People 2010*. Washington, DC: US Department of Health and Human Services, 2000.

US Department of Health and Human Services. *Healthy People 2020*. Washington, DC: US Department of Health and Human Services, 2010.

US Department of Health and Human Services, Public Health Service. *Mental Health: A Report of the Surgeon General*. Rockville, MD: US Department of Health and Human Services, 1999.

US Department of Health and Human Services, Public Health Service, Office of the Surgeon General. *The Surgeon General's Call to Action to Prevent and Decrease Overweight and Obesity*. Rockville, MD: US Department of Health and Human Services, 2001.

World Health Organization. Online: http://www.who.int/.

– 7 –

Some Thoughts on Black Leadership

TAVIS SMILEY

IN HIS REVOLUTIONARY BOOK of 1903, *The Souls of Black Folk*, civil rights activist and author W. E. B. DuBois poses this controversial question: Would America have been America without her Negro people? Imagine for a moment living in this place called America without the contribution of Black leaders. It would be a world without jazz—without John Coltrane or Miles Davis or Wynton Marsalis. Traffic lights, invented by scientist Garrett Morgan, would not exist to keep your BMW from hitting my Benz at an intersection! Our African American sisters would be deprived of Madam C. J. Walker's cosmetic products! We would live in an America without peanut butter!

I can't even conceive of it. And I'm so glad I don't have to.

George Washington Carver and other Black pioneers, brave men and women, offered their service to America; a place that didn't always welcome it, a place that didn't always embrace it, a place that didn't always appreciate it. Whenever history has called on us—as it has many, many times—we have accepted the challenge to be the conscience of this country. That's what Black folk are, as I see it. We are the conscience of this country.

When haters stood behind anything and everything to defy and deny Black folk their equal rights—the United States Constitution, the Declaration of Independence, the Emancipation Proclamation, even God and the Bible—our people still stepped up to serve. During times of war, when African Americans were enslaved or segregated by this country, they still volunteered to serve and to fight and to die on her behalf. They weren't fighting for what America *was;* they were fighting for what America could *become.* That took courage. That took conviction. That took commitment. And, I believe, that is also the ultimate definition of patriotism. To me, that is what Black leadership is all about.

However, I confess that I have some ambivalence about the term "Black leadership." I'm ambivalent about the characterization. I'm ambivalent about those who attempt to label Black leadership. I'm ambivalent about those who feel it necessary to define Black leadership, and I'm ambivalent about the attempt to critique Black leadership. I recognize that our leadership style stems from our struggle, and for that reason it has its own flavor. But I am bothered that we allow others, specifically those in the media and in other positions of influence, to define this term, "Black leadership." Flowing from the lips of some, it becomes a term that is pejorative and intellectually punitive. When was the last time you heard the term "white leadership"? You've never heard it, and you never will because nobody critiques "white" leadership. We need to do a better job of checking these folk who are drawing these lines and making these distinctions as if "leadership" and "Black leadership" are two different things. I don't care what color you are, what gender you are, or what age you are: either you lead or you don't lead. If you think you're leading and nobody's following you, then you're just out for a walk! You're certainly not a leader.

James Baldwin, one of the most brilliant essayists that America—not just Black America—has ever known, explained the role of color in our society like this: "Color is not a human or personal reality; it is a political reality." Whether you like it or not, when you step into a position of leadership in this country, you represent the entire Black race. We are judged as a group, as if Black folk think monolithically, while white folk are evaluated as individuals, not as a race. It's not right, it's not fair, but that is the reality. As African Americans and as leaders, the stakes for our success are much higher than anyone else's. So when you have the opportunity to exercise leadership, you better bring your A-game, because if you fail, you deny future chances for other folk who look just like you.

I once read that there are no good times to be Black in America, and some times are worse than others. Now, I love being a Black man, and for all the money in the world you couldn't pay me to be anything else. But let's be real about it: when God was handing out colors, nobody would have volunteered to be Black if they knew what troubles lay ahead! There's a price we have to pay, there are bridges that we have to get across, there are obstacles we have to get around that are placed in our way just because God handed us more melanin.

A few years ago, there was a *Newsweek* magazine story that caused a lot of conversation, controversy, and consternation. The cover of the magazine proclaimed that now was a great time to be Black in America. When I saw that cover at the newsstands, I grabbed the magazine. I just had to know what they thought was so much better about being an African American today. The main point of the article was that now was a great time to be Black in America *as compared to back in the day*. I don't think they had any Negro leaders up in that room when they were writing this article. Without question, we live in a better time than in the brutal days of slavery and segregation. It doesn't take a rocket scientist to figure that out. *Newsweek* got the context all wrong. The true measure of our quality of life is in the comparison to today's white America, not yesterday's Black America. How good do we have it as Black folk *today* versus white folk? That is the real issue. Like Baldwin said, race is not a personal reality, race is not a human reality, race is a *political* reality.

Now we stand at an extraordinary crossroads. For the first time in Black America's history, we have rising leaders who did not come from the generation of the civil rights movement. Our emerging young leaders have no firsthand perspective on the defining moment of African American history. We question what Black America will look like a few years down the road, with new leaders who were not part of the movement. What kind of leadership will they provide, can they provide, absent that struggle?

This generation can't compare the "before" and "after" pictures; they only know the Black America in the "after" picture. They have the freedom and privilege to eat in any restaurant, attend any school, get any job they want because of the struggle of the Black leaders who came before them. They don't know what it means to be told no. Don't misunderstand me: racism is still alive and well and an intractable issue in this country. But today, African Americans are afforded countless opportunities that could never have been imagined during Dr. King's time. The central challenge facing these new leaders, facing all African Americans, is, how will our new leadership be developed, how will our new leadership be defined, how will our new leadership be measured?

I propose that we evaluate these Black leaders as we always have done, and that is to put them to the test. If they don't possess what I call the three Cs—courage, conviction, and commitment, in that order—they cannot be Black leaders. When we put today's Black leaders to this test, we see that some are passing and some are failing. It is essential that our new leaders have courage, conviction, and commitment. Black leadership is needed now more than ever.

Now, I am not saying that the leaders who pass this test will not have any failures. To be a leader is to sometimes fail. And as long as you are Black up in here, you sho' nuff going to have some failures. That great leader Benjamin Elijah Mays put it like this: "Not failure," said Mays, "not failure, but low aim is sin." It is up to the rest of us Black folk—and no one else—to make sure we have leaders who pass the test of the three Cs.

This country is in trouble. There is a litany of issues, globally and domestically, inside of Black America and outside of Black America, that are going to challenge our leadership now and well into the future. As the conscience of this country, we have to be ready to step up again. The voice of Black leaders is going to matter, and in the eyes of many in this country, they will be speaking for all Black Americans. That is why it is imperative that we find and develop a qualified pool of talent from which to choose our leaders. The stakes are higher than ever. It is our responsibility to make sure our leaders are prepared.

For our brave new Black leaders, I offer some advice:

First: Don't let anybody ever tell you that the way to succeed is to transcend your race, to transcend who you are—not corporate America, not the government, and especially not the US Supreme Court. No. Embrace your race, embrace who you are, and be authentic. Our folks are craving authenticity in our leaders. I've learned that folk will not always agree with you, but they will always respect you if you are authentic.

Second: You have to be concerned about the least of us. Dr. King said that the most persistent and urgent question in life is, "What are you doing for others?" All of the folk in our history that we respect and admire and uplift are the folk who found a way to serve. Today we've got it all twisted. The way to be great is not to be popular, not to be famous, not be super rich. That's not how to earn respect. The way to get there is to love and to serve.

Finally, you have to be the best at whatever you do. If your lot in life is to be a street sweeper, you sweep the streets like Michelangelo painted the Sistine Chapel. You sweep the streets like Beethoven composed symphonies. You sweep the streets like Shakespeare wrote poetry. Be the best at whatever you do in this life.

I love the story of the gazelle and the lion. In the jungle, the scrawny gazelle wakes up everyday and starts running. Why? Because he knows that if he doesn't start the day by running, then later in the day, he's going to be somebody's lunch. The lion, king of the jungle though he may be, also wakes up everyday and starts running. Why? Because he knows if he doesn't wake up running, he will miss his chance to eat that gazelle for lunch, and he'll go hungry.

The moral of the story is that at the end of the day, it doesn't matter if you are the lion or the gazelle. Both wake up running to stay alive. Everyday we've got to wake up running, trying to find a way to make Black America better. In the great race of life, he who starts behind must forever remain behind or run faster than the man in front.

Brothers and sisters, it's time for us to pick up the pace.

– 8 –

The Decline of Friendship in Modernity: Issues and Challenges for Ethical Leadership

PRESTON KING

I DON'T COME TO you on purpose as a preacher, or even as a moralist. For more than forty years, I've been a poor academic, so you might expect me to present you with more of an argument than with any form of revelation. The argument, I suspect, slightly uncomfortably, is one you will not likely embrace. This is not because I don't think you will measure up. If we are going to go down that path, I certainly would not measure up. I have very serious doubts of my ability to persuade you of the truth of something that seems to me to be plain and pressing. So why do I expect you to resist? I expect you to resist for two principal reasons. First, the argument that I propose is not one that is usually heard. Second, it cuts right across what is usually heard, so there's a difficulty here.

The argument, very briefly, goes like this: In conditions of modernity, friendship has long been in decline. On balance, this probably can have a debilitating impact on the quality of contemporary life, and on the question of leadership.

To say that friendship has declined in modernity may sound a bit misleading. It may suggest that humans have changed in some very signal way, which seems somehow improbable. Didn't President Bill Clinton speak of basketball legend Michael Jordan as his friend? Didn't British Prime Minister Tony Blair address President Clinton as his friend? Didn't civil rights leader Andrew Young speak of Dr. Martin Luther King Jr. as his friend? These are very common usages, so we can't be altogether unaccustomed. Am I so destitute of friends as not to be aware of the problem that this sort of situation presents? There's a lot to think about here. So let me start by entering some exclusions.

First, I don't for a moment wish to say that there's absolutely no such thing as friendship among us. Obviously, there is friendship. If there was no friendship, we could not possibly be in a position to know what we were missing. So I have to assume that something of that sort does exist.

Second, I don't even claim that there isn't *a lot* of friendship among us. Often we are loyal without wanting to appear so, because loyalty, especially in certain circumstances, can be embarrassing. Who among us wants to be perceived as being loyal to some, where this might imply being an enemy to others? There is a tendency today, more than ever before, to back away from the notion of friendship because it is regarded as requiring compromise. But this does not mean that people do not have these sentiments.

My third and final exclusion: I don't even suggest that sometimes there may not be too much friendship, such as among thieves, gang members, Ku Klux Klansmen, Masons, Wall Street insiders, the rich, the powerful—whomever. We have that kind of constraint. In other words, there is some problem about limitations.

The argument is not that friendship has no downside. The point is that every ideal that you can possibly manipulate has a downside, even friendship. What is interesting is that the most significant downside for this society is that we have more or less abandoned friendship as an ideal in formal public discourse.

Let me now narrow my claim, having entered these exclusions. Friendship in modernity is specifically in decline compared to the role that it played among the ancients. Friendship has virtually disappeared from public philosophical debate and advocacy. In a distant past, friendship used to be the overarching ideal of all major thinkers and philosophers. It died a kind of ideological death. It did so at least among leaders and intellectuals, if not among people at large, as much as two thousand years ago. Today, even the memory of this ideological dominance is almost forgotten, especially among professional historians of ideas.

What is the evidence? Well, the evidence is fairly straightforward. It's simply a question of being prepared to look at it in the face. The evidence is essentially that virtually every major writer of ancient Greece and Rome had something celebratory to say about friendship. It was an ideal that wasn't just mindlessly trumpeted; it was one that was subject to convoluted, sophisticated political and philosophical analysis. Friendship, if you look at Plato's writings, is the linchpin of the entire system. Plato is platonic—not as is usually thought, by excluding love (Eros). He's platonic by seeing the erotic as a natural and indispensable platform on which enduring friendship is built. He sees friendship itself as a launching pad for the attainment of any abiding spiritual understanding. Plato's greatest book, *The Republic*, whether you regard it as misguided or not, essentially argues for the construction of government based upon some sense of fellowship among its members, or *koinonia*. That's what it's all about. We've been disposed to attack this notion, but it's quite clear that it is important in a figure like Plato and it caps the whole thrust of his work.

We usually make a distinction between Plato and Socrates, although it is difficult because of the actual historical connection between them. So far as we can reconstruct the position, Socrates has, in his famous words, "a passion for friends." We probably know him more for that formula than for any other. Friendship in the Socratic dispensation is the cement of society. It doesn't matter that friendship is restrictive. It has to be restrictive. Socrates can't be a friend to everybody, so there's a numerical restriction. A friend should not be incautious or careless in the formation of friendship, so there's a moral restriction. But Socrates does not limit the notion and prospect of friendship only to persons who are beautiful or free or rich or male. Wherever friendship emerges, in whatever form, among whatever strata, Socrates appears to see it overall as grounded in virtue, and the virtue, itself, grounded in a regard for the Other. That's the central picture that one gets from reading about this classic figure.

Xenophon, one of the great historians of antiquity, was one who very importantly wrote about Socrates. Xenophon claimed that friendship for Socrates was not at all a matter of abstract affection, emotion, or longing. Xenophon reported on a chance visit by Socrates to Theodota, an astonishingly beautiful woman, materially enriched by the favors of her friends. (To call her a prostitute would convey a disparagement that was as alien to Socrates as it would have been to Jesus.) The account that we are given of their encounter is very interesting. Always—*always*—Socrates seems burdened by a concern to give advice in a friendly and amicable way to Theodota, whom he appears genuinely to like. Socrates tells her that she "shouldn't spread her affections too thinly." You can almost hear him saying this on the page. He says Theodota should be selective in the friends that she attracts. She should work particularly hard at keeping good friends. She shouldn't manage them in such a way that they tire of her or that she tires of them.

This is not a fun thing for Socrates. It is clearly something that he feels quite immediately but quite profoundly, and it is not limited to whom it is that the person might be. There are no limits here. Socrates is not someone who is interested in greed, acquisition, or wealth. He is someone who is concerned with an empire of a mind. It's a very powerful force, not only among his contemporaries, but even in this present day, reaching down through the ages to us. If the Socrates whom Xenophon portrays is superbly moral and philosophical, he's not in any way superior or somber or detached. He's a funny kind of fellow and intensely intellectual, and he's moved, most importantly, by feeling. Nothing human is alien to him—absolutely nothing. He's full of practical advice, homespun examples. The abiding theme here is friendship, empathy, recognition of the Other, looking a person in the eye, wondering about them, being interested in them. The theme is friendship.

The interesting thing in the Socratic case is that the structure of friendship for him is always suffused with rational argument. The clear position is that in the case of friends, it is not the case that you avoid argument. That is what friendship is for. It is only among friends that you can argue, that you can feel free to express yourself fully, to develop an idea, to expect that people will not respond in an awkward, invidious, or painfully self-conscious kind of way. To this supremely rational man, that's what friends are for—not to become simple scientists, not to harden their look, not to become indifferent to what is going on. Having friends in whom you can invest your most precious thoughts and who can reciprocate is a way of becoming scientific, becoming rational.

This is the notion of friendship that is given currency by Socrates. But he builds upon something that is already there in early society, which says the most important thing is looking people in the face, shaking their hand, finding out what's going on, how they are feeling, what's happening on the farm.

In Books 8 and 9 of *The Nicomachean Ethics*, Aristotle is equally absorbed by friendship, but in a very different way than Socrates. Where

Socrates sees love and friendship as naturally intertwined, Aristotle introduces the notion of the superiority of abstract reason over brute passion. For some commentators this is the beginning of the end, and should never have happened.

It isn't the case that Aristotle abandons the notion of friendship. It always remains core, even in the analysis of politics. He categorizes different governments both in terms of the nature of the ruler and the kind of empathy the ruler has for his people. For example, a key distinction for Aristotle is between a monarch, who is an okay guy, and a tyrant, who is not. But what's the real difference between them? The monarch, at least, rules in the interest of his people. The tyrant does not. The tyrant does not understand his people. He has no interest in them. He cannot talk to them. He cannot move among them. The tyrant is bound to be an unhappy person ruling over an unhappy flock.

This concept of friendship, even when Aristotle begins to intrude some serious doubts about how intellectual one can be while remaining a friend, still retains the notion of relationship, of connecting with other people, as absolutely vital to any civilizing project. That's the point. Aristotle could not understand what we might call "civilization" as existing without friendship. When Aristotle famously characterizes man as a political animal, what he means is simply that people are nothing without friendship. This was a part of his science. When Aristotle claims that a person without a city, without a community, is either a god or a beast, again he means that if you haven't got friends you may be more than human, you may be less than human, but you can't quite be one of us. Humanity is nothing without friendship, without relation, without empathy, without a sense of connection.

The broad conclusion is fairly clear, right? Friendship was the dominant paradigm of Antiquity. Do not be misled with talk about liberty; to be so misled would be a great mistake. You see, we think we can see the past very clearly. Too often, we read the past in terms of what we think is valuable. In our Western tradition, liberty for us is absolutely essential. Therefore, projecting into the past, we think liberty must have been central for people like Plato and Aristotle, and we are just wrong. That's not the way it works. Their focus is very different from our focus. Friendship is their bandwagon. They all get on board. They aren't doing it in a party-political way. They are arguing with it, they are caught up in it. It isn't a simplistic doctrine that you can boil down and pass out as sweets to a flock that wants to be pacified. No, these folks are conducting an argument, but the framework, the paradigm, the ideological construct, is friendship.

Ancient theory, according to Aristotle, does not pitch upon an individual, as it does in the social contract theories from the seventeenth century onward, with which we have become most familiar. It pitches instead upon a relationship: you and I, him and her, boy and girl, old and young, teacher and pupil, us and them. In ancient theory, there is always a relationship. It is not the isolated individual that matters; it is the *connectedness* that matters. The social analysis of the Ancients conventionally focuses upon individuals in a relationship, not upon individuals as islets, as separate, autonomous creatures. The model of a good relation is always some notion of friendship. Ego is persistently linked to and enthused by some effective alter. Everything turned on these relationships. Wasn't it wonderful? X gave himself for Y, etc. This was what mattered, this was the spiritual realization recited in all of these ties, in all of these combinations: Horace and Virgil, Achilles and Patroclus, always this tie, this relational notion. The ideal that is celebrated is not so much the conquest of new worlds, not even in the case of Alexander the Great. Whatever the action or behavior, the priority—conceptually, ideologically—is always conceded to spiritual accord; not of accord with God, in this case, but with some significant Other, in which that Other, for each, is as valuable as you are yourself entering into it. Here you have some sort of notion of relatedness, and associated with that, selflessness—although there is a lot of argument about how far that can, or should, go. Usually the argument is for reciprocity; that you always get something in relation to something that you give.

The idea of friendship in the ancient world is not, as sometimes thought, an exclusively male construct. It is a male construct, but not exclusively so. Ancient Greek tradition supplies any number of classic cases of idealized heterosexual affection. Orpheus and Eurydice, Hero and Leander, Sappho and Alcaeus, Hecuba and Priam, Odysseus and Penelope. The pairs are as much heterosexual as they are not, and all are based on the idea that friendship is the tie that matters.

That emphasis in the Ancient world makes that world much, much, much, much more alien than we might at first suppose. If you think of one tradition, and if you think just for a moment how different that tradition is, it isn't really so close as you might imagine, because our world tends to be locked into a very different set of constructs. Here we are to do with a pretty fierce embrace of liberty, choice, self-assertion, individuality, and similar virtues. Let's not knock it. Let's just take note of the difference. It's a very significant difference. If we inspect the modern period, the disposition we most commonly encounter with regard to friendship, at least among our intelligencias, is one ranging from indifference to suspicion to hostility. The prejudices and conclusions of major thinkers are not necessarily embodied in the social practice of ordinary people. In the Modern period, we immediately detect a sharp divergence from Ancient predecessors. Virtually none of the major Modern thinkers is to do with the embrace of, praise of, analysis of, friendship—not Machiavelli, not René Descartes, not Thomas Hobbes, Barclay, David Hume, Voltaire, not even Jean-Jacques Rousseau, certainly not John Stewart Mill, least of all Jeremy Bentham, and not Georg Hegel, not even Karl Marx. None of these people is concerned with the construct of friendship.

Increasingly, as we get into the Modern period and the ideas of science, something begins to get elided. Either this notion doesn't sit well with the love of God and gets extruded for that reason, or it doesn't sit well with a new calm, rationalistic sort of scientism. But in any event, the effect tends to be the same. You see it celebrated in Mary Shelley's *Frankenstein*. Dr. Frankenstein suddenly is a monster. What is the monster? It's the rationality in the Modern age. And what is Dr. Frankenstein up to? He wants to explore new worlds all on his own. He does it secretly, in a closet. He has no mates. He has a wife, but the great thing about his wife is that she doesn't know what the good doctor is up to, and he thinks that is all for the better. He is the great scientist with graying hair and a changing mien who will alter the world, but now in this highly individuated form. Frankenstein is a sort of symbol of modernity, that notion of the person always in some species of communion. The German sociologist Herman Schmalenbach put it in those terms: "communion" with another or others; the idea of a person as always achieving moral value through valuing some other or others as their own highest end. All of that somehow dissolves into a later notion of the person as free and self-subsistent, perhaps even empowered.

But the notion of friendship basically tends to sink, and you can almost see it there. It's odd. You wonder why, and you can't quite come to grips with it. You can explain it only in retrospect. It's very easy with hindsight to explain anything, isn't it? All we can say with certainty is that the concept of friendship *does* sink. It is like a waterlogged boat, lovely as it might have been. It just sinks and we don't quite know why. The individual emerges from the bog of nature through the pursuit of self-interested ends, through the maximization of personal utilities. We, increasingly in this economistic sort of terminology, begin to formulate what the purpose of persons is. Largely it tends to turn around a highly individuated self-realization, which can be good because it can empower society if everyone is doing his own thing.

But friendship was the prism through which the ancients perceived the workings of nature. It was through this prism that they understood the purpose of life, and it was through this construct that they had some sense of the proper functioning of society. The friendship paradigm for them was construed as much more an affect of science than a mere matter of morality. Of course, it was a powerful matter of morality for them because it shaped a distinct sense of what one should or should not do.

Now I want to enter into the analysis of what the notion of friendship might actually reduce to so that we might more clearly see the relationship between ancient notions and present notions. The ancients focused more upon relationship than upon individuality. But it's clear that we could, as you might say they did, articulate relationship in at least four ways: male to female, male to male, female to female, and I to I (or me to me, or me to myself). The ancients basically focus on the first three. Our focus is wholly on the fourth, to the exclusion of the others. It's interesting to follow that through to see how it goes.

That fourth relationship is a very vexed one. If love is a relationship, there's a question as to how far it may be possible to enjoy such a relationship with oneself. It's an awkward one. The few cases that we have of children who have grown up in the wild, alone, suggest that they had no deep sense of love for others, but equally, no keen self-awareness. This suggests that even the notion of egoism or egotism is actually a social construct. You cannot pretend that it's just a given, just there, that it's natural, as many of the Utilitarians want to argue. You cannot pretend that because our empirical experience points in exactly the other direction. If you leave people alone in an unsocial state, they have no sense of who they might be, no sense of how to relate, and most importantly, no sense of self. It's very difficult to contend with individuality in this sort of self-subsistent way, as being a nonsocialized construct.

So that fourth relationship of I to I, me to me, me to myself, is conventionally construed by the Ancients as a matter of self-love. But most revealingly, when you look at how they deal with it, what you see is that they tend to summarize the whole idea in the story of Narcissus. That's how they deal with it. Narcissus is sick. Narcissus is wandering through some lonely glade when he happens to cast his glance into a pond and see a reflection of himself. What a fair, handsome boy, he thinks, and falls in love with himself. Narcissus pines away until he dies because the one self that he cannot really consummate his affection with, the one self that he cannot wed himself to, is himself. For the Ancients it's a failure, which means that this forced relationship is virtually incomprehensible to them. It is not something they can understand. It is not a question of despotism, it's not a question of people not arguing things out. You won't find tighter arguments than in Socrates and Plato and Aristotle. But they are oriented from the notion of friendship rather than individuality.

One consequence of this belief in friendship is the firm tendency to exclude the possibility of explaining the behavior of others as evil. Now that's an interesting check. Don't worry about how people may actually behave: yes, they kill one another and they rape one another, but who doesn't, you know? Yes, we know people do these things and it's dreadful. It's very difficult for them, given this relationality concept, to explain such behavior in terms of an evil Other. They cannot deal with the human world in this context in terms of evil. They cannot deal with others as evil. The Other in this construct is some probable extension of oneself. The Other may do one harm, but possibly no more harm than you will do yourself. We have heard, at least, of self-destruction. That's a very real option. The whole notion of tragedy in Greek discourse is precisely self-destruction. There's a built-in disinclination to explain your failures in terms of what somebody else has done to you. There may be all sorts of explanations, but evil won't cut it. So you tend to get, in explaining human behavior, much more suppleness. This does have policy implications. I don't want to belabor that. It becomes much more complex. But one of the things that a friendship construct tends to exclude is the notion of the evil Other.

What's distinctive about the twentieth century, in particular, extending backwards to key thinkers in the nineteenth century, is the tendency to embrace this fourth construct—I to I, me to me, me to myself—and render it more important than all the rest. The ancients would see anything like an exclusive focus on your relationship with yourself, your individuality, as more pathological than not. We, by contrast, are disposed to see I to I, so to speak, with the notion of being pals to ourselves. And so equally, at the extreme of individuating ourselves from other selves and ceasing to be able to understand them, and at the extreme, theorizing their behavior as so totally alien as to be evil.

You can spot the nature of this difference between the friendship and liberty paradigms in the fact that one tends to point toward a duty of self-lessness, where the other points to a duty of self-realization. Each is important, but they don't blend too lumplessly in your moral mixer. You can take them together but it's difficult to smooth out the differences.

Consider a figure like Odysseus. He's no romantic. He's obsessed by a sense of a duty to return to his family, to his wife, Penelope. But the hero, for example, in author Stephen Crane's *The Red Badge of Courage*, is not seeking another Self. He's our sort of romantic. He's in search of himself in the heart of darkness. The hero or antihero is rather similar.

In much of our modern writing, the heroes are essentially in pursuit of themselves. Consider the works of F. Scott Fitzgerald, Ernest Hemingway, Richard Wright, James Baldwin. The heroes are the cowboy type: Tom Mix, Roy Rogers, Gene Autrey, John Wayne, Clint Eastwood. This cowboy performs stellar deeds, then rides off into the sunset, alone. There may be a pleasant uncertainty associated with all this, but he's detached. He doesn't get tied up, and he doesn't get tied down. Modern heroes classically tend to be loners; ancient heroes are not. Travis Bickle, Robert DiNiro's character in *Taxi Driver*—a loner. He may come good, he may come bad, but either way, he'll come alone. Some heroes have sidekicks—the Lone Ranger has Tonto, Batman has Robin, Tarzan even has Jane—but they don't really have pals, they don't have partners. They stand on their own.

Typically, when we seek freedom for, say, African slaves in America, we don't seek to include them, but only to detach them from a specifically personal dependency. The idea is that they, too, should figuratively or physically ride off into the sunset. When we seek freedom for women, we're less likely to seek reevaluation of caring as a vital social role, but more to open up careers to self-realization through power seeking. Now, if you think this is turning into a diatribe against feminism, forget it. Thank God for feminism. But spot the direction that our own overarching cultural value tends to impose upon it. Freedom for women has tended, among ourselves, given our values, to dictate that women become more like men, not men more like women; that women wear trousers, not that men not wear skirts; that women become coarser, not men gentler; that women too in the end, mount up and ride off alone into the TV set, munching on a Big Mac. Now that's not just my opinion. Feminist movement leaders Betty Friedan and Germaine Greer push that argument. They are worried. What they are seeing is that one of the ways in which their movement is being pushed is simply in terms of this individuation, this breaking up of relationships, this paring away of something emotive that they had thought would be of value.

For major figures in our period—philosopher Immanuel Kant, psychologist Sigmund Freud, novelist Ayn Rand, anthropologist Mary Douglas—anything that distracts from attention to the I/I relationship is a moral travesty to be resisted at all costs. Our key doctrine is freedom, self-containment, self-realization, choice, more choice, the market, freedom of the market, privacy, and yes, private power, but power all the same. We do sanction the domination of others in the modern age, but we do it indirectly through the power that possession and privatization will secure. It's foolish, I suggest, to see evil in this. If you believe that ideas control the lives of people, you can see one way in which our behaviors are a function of extreme applications of our beliefs, and everyone is caught up in what he or she believes. These beliefs constitute a dominant outlook in our period, and it's very difficult to escape them. We're born with them. The question is how possible it is to begin to make adjustments that accommodate them.

Let me say this: every construct that becomes a dominant paradigm, if you push it hard enough, will be seen to have flaws. It will have difficulties of which we shall need to take account. One of the things that we see looking back historically is the way in which one major construct dominant at a given time has been almost entirely removed from the calendar of events and replaced by something else; something important, something valuable. It's not all bad. Let's not commit a mistake by running in the other direction.

The point here is this: are we to be governed simply by abstract ideas in one form? Or do we step back and think every theory runs up against its limits, and we have to use our minds, our judgment, sometimes in the application of other theories. I put it to you that something like friendship is not an important ideal to conjure with. Don't just think of the Klu Klux Klan or Nazis or of other people who misuse the *we* relationship. But there are limits that apply in the case of the other notions by which we happen to be bound.

I will conclude with a bad joke. It has to do with a preacher who's absolutely persuaded that he knows full well what the will of God is, that he's a loyal servant and that he knows for certain what divine providence should dictate. This good man builds a house, believing it is God's will that he should do so. He makes it imminently livable, thinking this, too, is an expression of God's will.

One day it starts to rain. Sometimes rain can strike with a certain desperation, and his house is hit hard. The floodwaters rise. His neighbors come by in a boat and say, "You must come away with us. You'll drown if you stay here." He reassures them that he knows God's will, and certainly God will not let him drown.

The waters continue to rise. He moves to the roof and a helicopter comes to take him away. Again he insists that he is in God's hands and all will turn out spiffingly.

But he drowns, and he's a little bit upset about it. When he enters heaven, he goes to see God straightaway. The man says to God, "How could you possibly treat me like this? I've been so loyal a servant! I've had such faith in you! How could you let me die in such a way?" And God says, without a trace of exasperation, "I told you, twice."

The point here is that you must be careful about taking too much to heart truths that may seem to be self-evident. They may be less self-evident than you think.

www.ingramcontent.com/pod-product-compliance
Lightning Source LLC
Chambersburg PA
CBHW030902170426
43193CB00009BA/717